# Tower Air Fryer

## Cookbook for Beginners

Easy-to-Follow & Delicious Tower Air Fryer Recipes Make Cooking
Fun for Beginners and Have a Feast with Your Family

**Patrice Blandford**

# Table of Contents

# Introduction

The Tower Air Fryer cooking appliance allows you to cook delicious and healthy meals anytime and quickly. Nowadays, we're all busier and busier, with less time to prepare and cook food in the kitchen. We're also more aware of eating healthier (but no less delicious!) food.

Luckily for us, the Tower Air Fryer is a cooking appliance that requires less food prep and produces scrumptious food in less time. When life is too short for spending ages in the kitchen, this air fryer is your perfect kitchen companion. This device can cook almost anything you want and yields amazingly tasty food prepared in less time with fewer calories.

But if you're new to the world of air frying, you may be confused about how the Tower Air Fryer works. You may even worry about facing some problems while using it for the first time. You needn't worry! This air fryer is easy to use, with user-friendly buttons. Simply read this introduction and the air fryer's instruction manual before use, and you'll soon get the hang of it.

One of the best things about this appliance is that it's large enough to cater for a whole family thanks to its large capacity, meaning that you won't need to cook food in batches. Another plus is its intuitive control panel, from where you control the cooking time and temperature. It also includes helpful accessories like an air fryer basket, cooking tray, and racks. Using the Tower Air Fryer, you'll cook delicious, tender, juicy, and healthy food in less time.

Another great aspect is how simple the appliance is to clean; you don't have to deal with umpteen pots, pans, and other utensils. When the air fryer has cooled completely, wipe it inside and out with a damp cloth. The accessories can go right in the dishwasher. Now you can relax and enjoy more time to yourself or with your family instead of being tied to the kitchen.

In my cookbook, I've included many simple, quick-to-make Tower Air Fryer recipes for you. You'll learn how to prepare food and use the air fryer in unique ways, get safety tips, and learn solutions to any problems that may arise while cooking with your device.

Happy air frying!

## What Is the Tower Air Fryer?

Tower has the most extensive range of air fryers in the UK and guarantees to meet all its customers' air frying needs. It comes with Vortx technology and cooks food 30% faster than other air fryers.

A Tower Air Fryer works like a convection oven and yields fat-free meals, cooking food by circulating hot air around the food through a traditional convection mechanism. The hot air is created by a high-speed fan, producing crispy yet tender food, and there's an exhaust fan right above the cooking chamber. The internal pressure increases the temperature of the tower air fryer, which is controlled by the exhaust system.

With this air fryer, you'll use less oil for cooking, making it a far healthier option. The air fryer provides an even cooking temperature, ensuring the food is perfectly cooked with no overcooked or undercooked bits. So not only is your food good for you, but it's delicious, too! But there's more good news: the operating buttons are user-friendly, the air fryer produces no odour, and it's safe to use. Oh, and as it saves energy, allowing you to cook food within 15 minutes, it's environmentally friendly and saves you money.

## Benefits of Using the Tower Air Fryer

The Tower Air Fryer provides many benefits, making your life easier. Sitting on your kitchen counter, it uses high-speed fans to cook delicious food.

**Large capacity:**
The Tower Air Fryer has a large capacity and is perfect for the whole family. You don't need to prepare food in batches and can prepare pretty much any type of food you desire.

**Preserves nutrients:**
The air fryer's cooking process allows your food to retain essential nutrients and yields healthy and delicious meals.

**Healthier food:**
You only need to use a minimal amount of oil with the air fryer, making mealtime healthier. You can cook all of your favourite fried foods with 99% less fat but no less delicious, crispy or tender. Plus, the appliance saves you time and money. So it's healthy for your wallet, too!

**Low energy consumption:**
The Tower Air Fryer cooks food 30% faster than conventional ovens, meaning it uses less energy. You can save up to 50% in energy by switching to air fryer cooking.

**Safe and fast cooking:**
The Tower Air Fryer is safer and more environmentally friendly than most kitchen cookers, especially deep-fat fryers. It doesn't produce too much heat, steam, or troublesome smoke, and there's no risk of spilling or splashing oil like in traditional deep fryers. Plus, there's less risk of burning your meals.
As it works faster than other kitchen appliances and air fryers, you can spend less time in the kitchen. Most meals cooked in the air fryer will be ready in just 15 minutes.

**No hob or oven needed:**
The Tower Air Fryer has several cooking functions, and you won't need to use your hob or oven. It truly is a fantastic option for busy days when you need to cook something delicious and fast. Plus,

unlike your other kitchen appliances, it doesn't produce smoke or steam.

**Easy cleaning method:**
This appliance is super easy to clean, with removable parts and accessories that can be safely washed in the dishwasher. A word of caution: don't put the main unit in the dishwasher or submerge it in water. You can clean it inside and out using a damp cloth. Before cleaning, unplug the air fryer and let it cool completely.

**Versatility:**
As I've mentioned, the Tower Air Fryer has several cooking functions, making it incredibly versatile and capable of preparing many types of meals. Whether for breakfast, lunch, dinner, or a snack, you can create tasty meat, veggie, or dessert recipes simply and quickly.

**Vortx technology:**
The tower air fryer comes with Vortx technology, meaning it cooks food 30% faster than other air fryers.

**Minimal mess:**
Using a Tower Air Fryer, your whole kitchen will be less messy and stay clutter-free. You'll no longer need to worry about splattering oil or multiple dirty pots and pans. Plus, the air fryer basket is simple to clean as it's non-stick and dishwasher-safe.

**Adjustable temperature and timer:**
This appliance has adjustable temperature control from 80 °C to 200 °C. It has a 1-hour timer with an automatic shut-off feature for accurate cooking.

A good companion for busy cooks:
The Tower Air Fryer makes the perfect kitchen companion. You simply prepare your ingredients and add them to the air fryer basket/tray. Adjust the cooking time, temperature, and desired cooking function and start cooking.

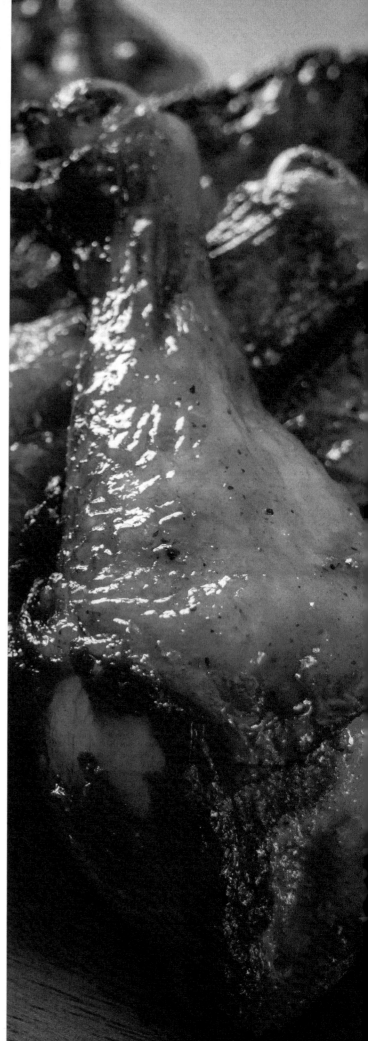

Firstly, remove and dispose of all the packaging, including from inside the main unit. Next, check the appliance to ensure there's no damage to the power cord, main unit, or accessories. Remove any labels. Clean the interior and exterior of the appliance with a damp cloth or non-abrasive sponge and a little washing-up liquid. Wipe it dry with a damp cloth. Either hand wash the accessories or put them in the dishwasher. Let them dry completely.

## The Control Panel

**Autocook Functions:**
The Tower Air Fryer's digital control panel contains all the buttons necessary to create your perfect meal, including eight autocook functions. (You can, however, adjust temperature and time.) These programmes are:

- **Steak**
- **Fries**
- **Drumsticks**
- **Fish**
- **Shrimp**
- **Roast chicken**
- **Rotisserie**
- **Dried fruit**

**Other Features:**
The control panel also has a **Fan Indicator, Heating Indicator, Temperature Indicator** and **Timer Indicator.**

The **Temperature Up Key** allows you to adjust the cooking temperature according to the recipe instructions.

The **Temperature Down Key** allows you to decrease the cooking temperature according to the recipe instructions.

The **Light ON/OFF Key** allows you can turn the unit's inner light on or off.

The **ON/Pause Key** allows you to start or stop cooking as you desire.

The **Timer Up Button** allows you to increase the cooking time according to the recipe instructions.

The **Timer Down Button** allows you to decrease

the cooking time according to the recipe instructions.

## Using the Appliance

Using the Tower Air Fryer is super easy. Read these instructions, and you'll be an air frying pro in no time. Let's dig in!

### A removable door

The Tower Air Fryer has a removable door, which can be pulled away from the appliance when you want to clean it. Firstly, push the door down as far as it will go, approximately 70°. Then, push the grooved latch on the right-hand side of the hinge horizontally to release the door. When the door has been released, pull it down to separate it from the appliance. If you want to reinstall the door, align the edges of the door with the holes on either side of the hinge and then insert it into the body of the unit.

### Automatic switch off

The air fryer has a timer that automatically shuts off the unit when the timer reaches zero. To turn it off manually, press the down timer key until it displays zero.

Preparing for use

Put the appliance on a stable, horizontal and even surface. Remember: don't put the unit onto a non-heat-resistant surface. Pull the cord from the storage compartment located at the bottom of the unit. Don't fill the air fryer with oil or any other liquid. Don't put anything on top of the appliance, as this will disrupt airflow and affect the cooking process.

## Using the Accessories

The Tower Air Fryer comes with a complete set of accessories to help you create your ideal meal. These include:

**Drip tray:** this catches any fat or drippings, making cleaning easier
**Airflow racks:** these can be used when dehydrating, crisping or reheating food, such as fruit pieces or pizza
**Roasting spit:** use this when roasting meat or fish
**Handle:** this helps you safely take out the accessories from the appliance

## Step-by-Step Air Frying

Using the Tower Air Fryer is super simple. Here is step-by-step guidance; if you follow these instructions, you can easily prepare food for yourself and your family.

If you have a new air fryer, clean it first:

For initial use, you should clean the air fryer thoroughly. Remove the packaging and accessories from the air fryer cooking appliance. Place the air fryer basket and reversible tray into the dishwasher and clean it with warm soapy water. Remove any dust with a clean and soft cloth. Clean the main unit with a damp cloth. When all air fryer parts are dry, return them to the main unit.

### Select a recipe and read it through first:

Choose your desired recipe from the book and read it at least two times to familiarize yourself with the ingredients and instructions.

### Purchase fresh ingredients:

If you want the best results and to create healthier dishes, buy fresh ingredients.

### Prepare your ingredients:

Before cooking, prepare all ingredients and measure them according to the recipe instructions. Cut vegetables to the same size to ensure they cook evenly. If you want to marinate any ingredients, make sure to give yourself time. If you're using frozen food, allow it to thaw if needed. Rinse the vegetables or fruits under running water and remove excess liquid before cutting.

**Spray the food with non-stick cooking spray:**
Purchase high-quality cooking spray and use it on your food before seasoning and placing it in the air fryer. This will ensure that the seasoning adheres to the food.

**Air Frying:**
Plug in the air fryer and open the appliance's door. Add the ingredients to the appropriate accessory, place it in the air fryer, and close the door. Open the tower air fryer door. Add ingredients into the air fryer basket using fetch the fork. Close the air fryer door.

The air fryer will make a beeping sound, and all the indicators will light up momentarily. After a few seconds, all of the indicators will go off except for the ON/Pause key, which will remain illuminated to indicate the appliance is turned on but in standby mode. Pressing this key while the air fryer is in this mode will bring up the touch control panel.

If no keys are pressed, or no modes are selected after the control panel is lit, the air fryer will automatically go into standby mode after 90 seconds of inactivity.

Select the desired cooking time according to the recipe instructions using the cooking time up or down keys. The time will increase or decrease in increments of 1 minute, from 0 up to 60 minutes.

Do the same for the temperature, using the temperature up or down keys. The temperature can be adjusted in increments of 5 °C, from 30 °C up to 200 °C.

**Note:** the timing and temperature can be changed at any time during the cooking process.

When you have selected the cooking time and temperature, press the On/Pause key. The electric heating tube and fan will start to work, and the fan and heating indicators will light up. The timer will start counting down the remaining cooking time.

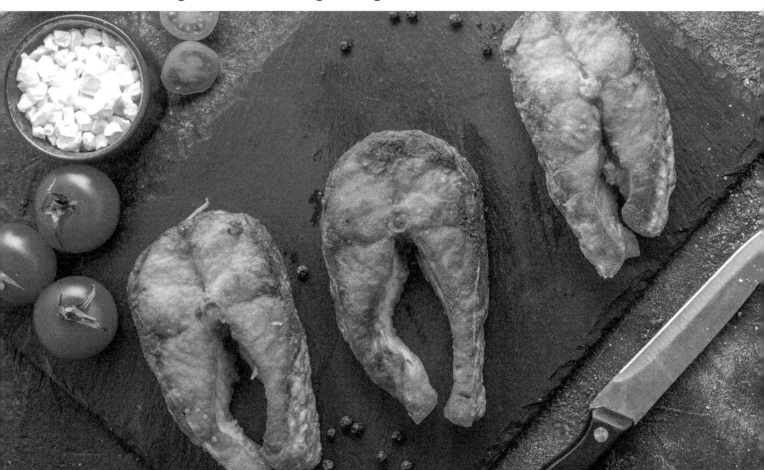

## Cooking Times and Temperatures for Various Recipes

| Meat and Poultry | Cooking Time (minutes) | Temperature (°C) |
| --- | --- | --- |
| Chicken breast | 10 to 15 | 180 |
| Drumsticks | 18 to 22 | 180 |
| Steak | 10 to 12 | 180 |
| Sausage roll | 13 to 15 | 200 |
| Pork chops | 8 to 12 | 180 |
| Hamburger | 10 to 15 | 180 |

| Snacks | Cooking Time (minutes) | Temperature (°C) |
| --- | --- | --- |
| Stuffed vegetables | 10 | 160 |
| Spring rolls | 8 to 12 | 200 |
| Frozen chicken nuggets | 6 to 10 | 200 |
| Frozen fish fingers | 6 to 20 | 200 |
| Frozen bread-crumbed cheese snacks | 8 to 10 | 180 |

| Baking | Cooking Time (minutes) | Temperature (°C) |
| --- | --- | --- |
| Sweet snacks | 20 | 160 |
| Muffins | 15 to 18 | 200 |
| Cake | 20 to 25 | 160 |
| Quiche | 20 to 22 | 180 |

| Fries and Potatoes | Cooking Time (minutes) | Temperature (°C) |
| --- | --- | --- |
| Potato gratin | 15 to 18 | 200 |
| Thin frozen fries | 9 to 16 | 200 |
| Thick frozen fries | 11 to 20 | 200 |

**Foods and their cooking temperatures:**

**Fish:** 180 °C

**Chicken/turkey:** 190 °C

**Pork:** 190 °C

**Beef/lamb:** 200 °C

**Note:** Adjust timings according to the desired doneness.

**Weights and measures:**

| Imperial | Metric |
|---|---|
| ½ oz | 15g |
| 1 oz | 30g |
| 2 oz | 60g |
| 3 oz | 90g |
| 4 oz | 110g |
| 5 oz | 140g |
| 6 oz | 170g |
| 7 oz | 200g |
| 8 oz | 225g |
| 9 oz | 255g |
| 10 oz | 280g |
| 11 oz | 310g |
| 12 oz | 340g |
| 13 oz | 370g |
| 14 oz | 400g |
| 1lb | 450g |

Although cooking is an art, it can also be very simple. If you're a cooking newbie, you should follow these steps to make the process easier:

- Clean all utensils, bowls, and equipment before cooking. Clean your work surface and cutting board. Rinse your veggies and meat under clean water and pat them dry.
- Wear comfortable clothing while cooking. And if you wear an apron, you won't have to worry about getting dirty.
- Always read your recipe twice before cooking to familiarize yourself with the timings and instructions.
- Measure your ingredients according to the recipe instructions. Place your prepared ingredients separately into small bowls.
- Cook with kosher salt and sprinkle with sea salt for the best results.
- If you didn't find shallots, then onion or garlic work just as well.
- Don't rinse pasta before cooking it.
- Remove the thick and rough stems of leafy green with your hands.
- Keep your spices and herbs away from any heat source, or they'll lose their flavour.
- Store fresh herbs in a glass of water and place it in the fridge.
- To prevent watery eyes, cut off the root of the onion before slicing it.
- You can use an egg slicer to cut small fruits such as kiwis.
- Keep knives sharp.
- Freeze leftover tomato paste in ice cube containers.
- Cut butter into pieces and leave it out for 10 to 15 minutes at room temperature to soften.
- If you want to grate soft cheese, place it in the fridge for 30 minutes.
- Always taste your food before serving, then season it as necessary.

Although cleaning your Tower Air Fryer is simple, there are some rules you should follow:

- Using steel wire brushes, metal utensils, and abrasive sponges can damage the air fryer, and don't use these to remove leftover food from the air fryer basket.
- Don't put the air fryer in the dishwasher or immerse it in water. Its removable parts and accessories are dishwasher-safe.
- Before cleaning, unplug the air fryer from the mains.
- Clean the air fryer after every use. Before cleaning, allow the appliance to cool. Remove the accessories using oven gloves or tongs in case they're still hot.
- Use a damp cloth or non-abrasive sponge for cleaning the interior and outside of the air fryer.
- To remove grease from the air fryer basket, soak it overnight in warm and soapy water. The next day, it will be removed easily.
- Use a soft scrub brush, washing-up liquid, baking soda, and a clean cloth for deep cleaning.

**To deep clean the air fryer:**

- Unplug the appliance and allow it to cool for 30 minutes. Remove the pan and basket from the air fryer and wash them with hot water and soap. If you see grease on these parts, soak them in hot water for 10 minutes. Then, scrub with a non-abrasive sponge.
- Clean the basket's interior with washing-up liquid and wipe it with a damp cloth. Remove the door of the air fryer and rinse it under clean water.
- Wipe the appliance with a moist or damp cloth carefully.
- If you see stubborn residue on the basket,

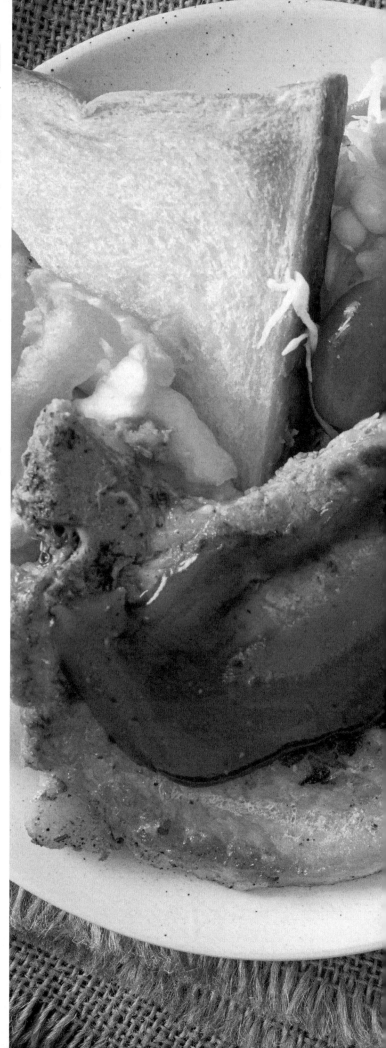

mix baking soda and water and scrub it into the grime with a soft brush.

- When all parts are dry, return them to the air fryer and reassemble the unit.

**Storing the Air Fryer:**

- Always clean the air fryer before storing it, ensuring that it's dried thoroughly. Store it in a dark, cool area on a flat, dry surface and out of reach of children.

## Helpful Tips

- For best results, remove the food from the air fryer immediately after cooking to avoid burning.
- Place the food into the air fryer basket in one layer to get tender and evenly browned food.
- Don't touch the surface of the appliance while cooking food. Use oven mitts or tongs.
- Adjust the desired temperature and cooking time on the display screen during any point of the cooking process, if necessary.
- When you open the door during cooking, the timer will pause. When you close the door, the cooking time will resume.
- Avoid overcooking.
- Use 1 tablespoon of oil for cooking vegetables. Remember, you'll need to use little to no oil with this air fryer.
- Don't immerse the appliance in water.
- Don't overfill the basket with oil or liquid.
- Clean the appliance after every use.
- Check the voltage of the main circuit before operating the appliance.
- Turn the appliance off at the wall socket, then remove the plug from the socket when not in use or before cleaning the appliance.
- Don't let children use or play with the appliance.
- Don't use any extension cord with this appliance.
- Don't pull the plug out by the cord, or your appliance will become damaged.

**1. The air fryer isn't working**

Possible reasons: The appliance isn't completely plugged in. You haven't adjusted the time or temperature.

Solution: Unplug the air fryer from the socket and plug it in again. Adjust the time and temperature controls.

**2. The food isn't frying properly**

Possible reasons: The air fryer has been overfilled. The time and temperature settings are too low for the cooking function.

Solution: Cook the food in batches if your serving size is too large; smaller batches will fry more evenly. Adjust the temperature and times for air frying.

**Wiring Safety for the UK:**

The wires are labelled as follows:

Blue neutral [N] Brown live [L] Green or Yellow [Earth]

The wire labelled **brown** is a live wire and must be connected with the terminal marked **[L]**.

The wire labelled **green or yellow** must be connected with the terminal marked **[E]**.

The wire labelled **blue** is neutral and must be connected to the terminal marked **[N]**.

# 4-Week Meal Plan

## Week 1

### Day 1:
Breakfast: Caprese Breakfast Pizza with Mozzarella Pearls and Basil Leaves
Lunch: Sweet Brussels Sprouts
Snack: Air-Fryer Raspberry Brie
Dinner: Tasty Cajun Prawn and Veggies
Dessert: Ultimate Chocolate Bread Pudding

### Day 2:
Breakfast: Whole Wheat Breakfast Pita
Lunch: Delicious Roasted Carrots
Snack: Italian Toasted Ravioli
Dinner: Italian Chicken Thighs
Dessert: Gorgeous Marble Cheesecake

### Day 3:
Breakfast: Mushroom-and-Tomato Stuffed Hash
Lunch: Golden and Crispy Potato Balls
Snack: Italian Crispy Stuffed Olives
Dinner: Beef Taco Chimichangas
Dessert: Irresistible Honey-Roasted Pears

### Day 4:
Breakfast: Simple Whole Wheat Banana-Walnut Bread
Lunch: Classic Green Bean Casserole
Snack: Baked Jalapeño Poppers
Dinner: Delicious Fried Prawn
Dessert: Sweet Pineapple Cheese Wontons

### Day 5:
Breakfast: Low-Calorie Honey-Apricot Granola with Greek Yogurt
Lunch: Lemon Butter Asparagus
Snack: Cheese Pizza Pinwheels
Dinner: Chicken and Spinach Salad
Dessert: Unbeatable Gooey Lemon Bars

### Day 6:
Breakfast: Savory Potato Hash
Lunch: Quick Yeast Rolls
Snack: Air-Fryer Egg Rolls
Dinner: Sweet and Spicy Short Ribs
Dessert: Delicious Baked Apples

### Day 7:
Breakfast: Whole-Wheat Blueberry Breakfast Cobbler
Lunch: Great Southwest-Style Corn Cobs
Snack: Garlic Buffalo Chicken Meatballs
Dinner: Breaded Pork Chops
Dessert: Creamy Choco-berry Fudge Sauce

## Week 2

### Day 1:
Breakfast: Crispy French Toast Sticks
Lunch: Flavourful Sweet Roasted Carrots
Snack: Crispy Crab and Cream Cheese Wontons
Dinner: Wonderful Fried Catfish
Dessert: Delicious Macaroon Bites

### Day 2:
Breakfast: Low-Calorie Blueberry Muffins
Lunch: Delicious Garlic Bread
Snack: Cheese Clam
Dinner: Spiced Chicken Drumsticks
Dessert: Strawberry Yogurt

### Day 3:
Breakfast: Delicious Pepperoni Pizza Bread
Lunch: Roasted Yellow Beans with Tangy Tomatoes
Snack: Tuna and Beans Wonton Cups
Dinner: Beef Empanadas with Cheeses
Dessert: Chocolate Coconut Pudding

### Day 4:
Breakfast: Crunch Bacon Veggie Bread Pudding
Lunch: Crispy Roasted Gold Potatoes
Snack: Cheesy Crab Mushrooms
Dinner: Quick Lemon-Garlic Jumbo Scallops
Dessert: Cream Berries Layer Cake

### Day 5:
Breakfast: Delicious Breakfast Toast
Lunch: Delicious Roasted Cremini Mushrooms
Snack: Crunchy Chips with Salsa
Dinner: Herbed Sriracha Turkey
Dessert: Silky Chocolate Pudding with Raspberries

### Day 6:
Breakfast: Country-Style Gravy
Lunch: Easy Caponata
Snack: Tangy Tomatillo Salsa Verde
Dinner: Wine-Braised Chuck Roast
Dessert: Cranberry Cream

### Day 7:
Breakfast: Cooked Eggs with Nutty Kale Pesto & Olives
Lunch: Cheesy Broccoli Florets
Snack: Crispy Cheddar Cheese Wafers
Dinner: Italian Parmesan Breaded Pork Chops
Dessert: Courgette Bread

## Week 3

### Day 1:
Breakfast: Low-Calorie Baked Peach Oatmeal
Lunch: Cauliflower Chickpeas Salad
Snack: Fried Chicken Wings
Dinner: Tropical Coconut Prawns
Dessert: Flavoured Vanilla Scones

### Day 2:
Breakfast: Breakfast Burritos
Lunch: Roasted Green Beans with Cheese and Pistachio
Snack: Cinnamon Pita Chips
Dinner: Crispy Chicken Tenderloins
Dessert: Lime Almond Pie

### Day 3:
Breakfast: Cheesy Butternut Squash Frittata
Lunch: Cheesy Beetroot
Snack: Cheese Crab Toasts
Dinner: Spicy Chuck Eye Roast with Tomatoes
Dessert: Poppy Seed Muffins

### Day 4:
Breakfast: Coconut Omelet with Nutmeg
Lunch: Chinese-Style Spiced Brussels Sprouts
Snack: Cumin Aubergine Fries
Dinner: Delicious Crab Croquettes
Dessert: Coconut Pie

### Day 5:
Breakfast: Cheese Veggie Frittata with Avocado Dressing
Lunch: Italian-Style Aubergine Fries
Snack: Crispy Apple Wedges
Dinner: Turkey Taquitos with Salsa
Dessert: Raspberry Tart

### Day 6:
Breakfast: Quick Mascarpone Omelet
Lunch: Herbed Cauliflower
Snack: Curried Sweet Potato Fries
Dinner: Delicious Beef Broccoli Patties
Dessert: Almonds Doughnuts

### Day 7:
Breakfast: Pork Lettuce Wraps
Lunch: Crispy Steak Fries with Toum
Snack: Kale Chips with Yogurt Sauce
Dinner: French Style Pork Chops
Dessert: Oatmeal-Carrot Cups

## Week 4

### Day 1:
Breakfast: Cinnamon Bagels
Lunch: Fried Pickles
Snack: Thai-Style Cauliflower Bites
Dinner: Air Fryer Salmon with Creamy Sauce
Dessert: Cinnamon Crisps

### Day 2:
Breakfast: Raisin Granola Bars
Lunch: Herbed Mushroom Frittata
Snack: Worcestershire Cheese Bread Bowl
Dinner: Crispy Chicken Drumsticks with Chives
Dessert: Maple Chocolate Chip Cookies

### Day 3:
Breakfast: Baked Avocado Egg Boat
Lunch: Croquettes of Fried Squash
Snack: Fried Crusted Cheese Ravioli
Dinner: Spicy Herbed Filet Mignon
Dessert: Frosted Chocolate Cake

### Day 4:
Breakfast: Banana-Nut Muffins
Lunch: Sweet Potatoes Glazed in Tamarind
Snack: Apricots and Cheese in Blankets
Dinner: Crab Legs with Lemon Butter Dip
Dessert: Enticing Caramelized Apples

### Day 5:
Breakfast: Pumpkin and Walnut Muffins
Lunch: Roasted Cauliflower with Pepper Jack Cheese
Snack: Savory Tater Tot Kebabs
Dinner: Peppercorns Chicken Breasts
Dessert: Delightful Apple Crisp

### Day 6:
Breakfast: Vegetable Bacon Hash
Lunch: Spicy Cauliflower Balls
Snack: Pesto Bruschetta
Dinner: Sherry-Braised Ribs with Grape Tomatoes
Dessert: Apple Cinnamon Puffs

### Day 7:
Breakfast: Classic Dijon Scotch Eggs
Lunch: Spicy Corn on Cob
Snack: Breaded Prawn Toast
Dinner: Pork Stuffed Peppers with Cheese
Dessert: Strawberry Puffs with Cashew Sauce

# Chapter 1 Breakfast Recipes

# Whole Wheat Breakfast Pita

**Prep Time: 5 minutes | Cook Time: 6 minutes | Serves: 2**

1 whole wheat pita
2 teaspoons olive oil
½ shallot, diced
¼ teaspoon garlic, minced
1 large egg

¼ teaspoon dried oregano
¼ teaspoon dried thyme
⅛ teaspoon salt
2 tablespoons shredded Parmesan cheese

1. Preheat the air fryer to 195°C. 2. Brush the top of the pita with olive oil, then spread the diced shallot and minced garlic over the pita. 3. Crack the egg into a suitable bowl or ramekin, and season it with oregano, thyme, and salt. 4. Place the pita into the air fryer basket, and gently pour the egg onto the top of the pita. Sprinkle with cheese over the top. 5. Bake for 6 minutes. 6. Allow the pita to cool for 5 minutes before cutting into pieces for serving.
**Per Serving:** Calories 126; Fat 8.52g; Sodium 312mg; Carbs 8.94g; Fibre 1.1g; Sugar 0.18g; Protein 4.18g

# Caprese Breakfast Pizza with Mozzarella Pearls and Basil Leaves

**Prep Time: 5 minutes | Cook Time: 6 minutes | Serves: 2**

1 whole wheat pita
2 teaspoons olive oil
¼ garlic clove, minced
1 large egg
⅛ teaspoon salt

55 g diced tomato
30 g mozzarella pearls
6 fresh basil leaves
½ teaspoon balsamic vinegar

1. Preheat the air fryer to 195°C. 2. Brush the top of the pita with olive oil, then spread the minced garlic over the pita. 3. Crack the egg into a small bowl or ramekin and season it with salt. 4. Place the pita into the air fryer basket, and gently pour the egg onto the top of the pita. Top with the tomato, mozzarella pearls, and basil. 5. Bake for 6 minutes. 6. Remove the pita pizza from the air fryer and drizzle balsamic vinegar over the top. 7. Allow to cool for 5 minutes before cutting into pieces for serving.
**Per Serving:** Calories 198; Fat 7.46g; Sodium 225mg; Carbs 28.56g; Fibre 5.2g; Sugar 1.06g; Protein 5.44g

# Low-Calorie Honey-Apricot Granola with Greek Yogurt

**Prep Time: 10 minutes | Cook Time: 30 minutes | Serves: 6**

85 g rolled oats
65 g dried apricots, diced
30 g almond slivers
30 g walnuts, chopped
30 g pumpkin seeds
40 g hemp hearts
85 to 110 g raw honey, plus more for drizzling

1 tablespoon olive oil
1 teaspoon ground cinnamon
¼ teaspoon ground nutmeg
¼ teaspoon salt
2 tablespoons sugar-free dark chocolate chips (optional)
735 g nonfat plain Greek yogurt

1. To prepare, heat your air fryer to 125°C. Line parchment paper over the air fryer basket. 2. Combine the oats, apricots, almonds, walnuts, pumpkin seeds, hemp hearts, honey, olive oil, cinnamon, nutmeg, and salt in a large bowl, mixing so that the honey, oil, and spices are well distributed. 3. Pour the mixture onto the parchment paper and spread it into an even layer. 4. Bake for 10 minutes, then shake or stir and spread back out into an even layer. Continue baking for 10 minutes more, then repeat the process of shaking or stirring the mixture. Bake for an additional 10 minutes before removing from the air fryer. 5. Allow the granola to cool completely before stirring in the chocolate chips (if using) and pouring into an airtight container for storage. 6. For each serving, top 120 g Greek yogurt with 60 g granola and a drizzle of honey, if needed.
**Per Serving:** Calories 171; Fat 8.19g; Sodium 157mg; Carbs 28.11g; Fibre 4g; Sugar 14.91g; Protein 5.27g

# Mushroom-and-Tomato Stuffed Hash

**Prep Time: 10 minutes | Cook Time: 20 minutes | Serves: 4**

Olive oil cooking spray
1 tablespoon plus 2 teaspoons olive oil, divided
100 g mushrooms, diced
1 spring onions, white parts and green parts, diced
1 garlic clove, minced

300 g shredded potatoes
½ teaspoon salt
¼ teaspoon black pepper
1 Roma tomato, diced
55 g shredded mozzarella

1. To prepare, heat your air fryer to 195°C. Lightly spritz the inside of a 15 -cm cake pan with olive oil cooking spray. 2. Heat 2 teaspoons olive oil over medium heat in a small frying pan. Add the mushrooms, spring onion, and garlic, and cook for 4 to 5 minutes, or until they have softened and are beginning to show some colour. Remove from heat. 3. Meanwhile, combine the potatoes, salt, pepper, and the remaining tablespoon olive oil in a large bowl. Toss until all potatoes are well coated. 4. Pour half of the potatoes into the bottom of the cake pan. Top with the mushroom mixture, tomato, and mozzarella. Spread the remaining potatoes over the top. 5. Bake in the air fryer for 12 to 15 minutes, or until the top is golden brown. 6. Remove from the air fryer and allow to cool for 5 minutes before slicing and serving.
**Per Serving:** Calories 179; Fat 1.6g; Sodium 406mg; Carbs 36.54g; Fibre 5.6g; Sugar 2.24g; Protein 9.05g

# Simple Whole Wheat Banana-Walnut Bread

**Prep Time: 10 minutes | Cook Time: 23 minutes | Serves: 6**

Olive oil cooking spray
2 ripe medium bananas
1 large egg
60 g nonfat plain Greek yogurt
60 ml olive oil
½ teaspoon vanilla extract

2 tablespoons raw honey
120 g whole wheat flour
¼ teaspoon salt
¼ teaspoon baking soda
½ teaspoon ground cinnamon
30 g chopped walnuts

1. To prepare, heat your air fryer to 180°C. Lightly coat the inside of an 20-by-10-cm loaf tin with olive oil cooking spray. (Or use two smaller loaf tins) 2. Mash the bananas with a fork in a large bowl. Add the egg, yogurt, olive oil, vanilla, and honey. Mix until well combined and mostly smooth. 3. Sift the whole wheat flour, salt, baking soda, and cinnamon into the wet mixture, then stir until just combined. Do not overmix. 4. Gently fold in the walnuts. 5. Pour into the prepared loaf tin and spread to distribute evenly. 6. Place the loaf tin in the air fryer basket and bake for 20 to 23 minutes, or until golden brown on top and a toothpick inserted into the centre comes out clean. 7. Allow the bread to cool for 5 minutes before serving.
**Per Serving:** Calories 237; Fat 12.6g; Sodium 296mg; Carbs 29.93g; Fibre 3.5g; Sugar 10.79g; Protein 4.06g

# Savory Potato Hash

**Prep Time: 15 minutes | Cook Time: 18 minutes | Serves: 6**

2 medium sweet potatoes, peeled and cut into 2.5 cm cubes
½ green pepper, diced
½ red onion, diced
100 g mushrooms, diced
2 tablespoons olive oil

1 garlic clove, minced
½ teaspoon salt
½ teaspoon black pepper
½ tablespoon chopped fresh rosemary

1. To prepare, heat your air fryer to 195°C. 2. Toss the sweet potato cubes, pepper, onion, mushrooms, olive oil, garlic clove, salt, black pepper, and the chopped fresh rosemary together in a large bowl until the vegetables are well coated and seasonings distributed. 3. Pour the vegetables into the air fryer basket, making sure they are in a single even layer. (If using a smaller air fryer, you may need to do this in two batches.) 4. Cook for 9 minutes, then toss or flip the vegetables. Cook for 9 minutes more. 5. Transfer to a serving bowl or individual plates and enjoy.
**Per Serving:** Calories 141; Fat 4.79g; Sodium 211mg; Carbs 24.73g; Fibre 3.7g; Sugar 3.89g; Protein 2.74g

# Low-Calorie Blueberry Muffins

**Prep Time: 10 minutes | Cook Time: 15 minutes | Serves: 6**

Olive oil cooking spray
120 g unsweetened applesauce
85 g raw honey
120 g nonfat plain Greek yogurt
1 teaspoon vanilla extract
1 large egg

190 g plus 1 tablespoon whole wheat flour, divided
½ teaspoon baking soda
½ teaspoon baking powder
½ teaspoon salt
75 g blueberries, fresh or frozen

1. To prepare, heat your air fryer to 180°C. Lightly coat the inside of six silicone muffin cups or a six-cup muffin tin with olive oil cooking spray. 2. Combine the applesauce, honey, yogurt, vanilla, and egg in a large bowl, and mix until smooth. 3. Sift in the flour, the baking soda, baking powder, and salt into the wet mixture, then stir until just combined. 4. Toss the blueberries with the remaining 1 tablespoon flour in a small bowl, then fold the mixture into the muffin batter. 5. Divide the mixture evenly among the prepared muffin cups and place into the basket of the air fryer. Bake for 12 to 15 minutes, or until golden brown on top and a toothpick inserted into the middle of one of the muffins comes out clean. 6. Then allow the muffins to cool for 5 minutes before serving.

**Per Serving:** Calories 184; Fat 1.63g; Sodium 303mg; Carbs 40.63g; Fibre 3.8g; Sugar 18.11g; Protein 4.63g

# Low-Calorie Baked Peach Oatmeal

**Prep Time: 5 minutes | Cook Time: 30 minutes | Serves: 6**

Olive oil cooking spray
165 g certified gluten-free rolled oats
480 ml unsweetened almond milk
85 g raw honey, plus more for drizzling (optional)
120 g nonfat plain Greek yogurt

1 teaspoon vanilla extract
½ teaspoon ground cinnamon
¼ teaspoon salt
230 g diced peaches, divided, plus more for serving
(optional)

1. To prepare, heat your air fryer to 195°C. Lightly spritz the inside of a 15 cm cake pan with olive oil cooking spray. 2. Mix together the oats, almond milk, honey, yogurt, vanilla, cinnamon, and salt in a large bowl until well combined. 3. Fold in 115 g of the peaches and then pour the mixture into the prepared cake pan. 4. Sprinkle the remaining peaches across the top of the oatmeal mixture. Bake in the air fryer for 30 minutes. 5. Allow to set and cool for 5 minutes before serving with additional fresh fruit and honey for drizzling, if desired.

**Per Serving:** Calories 221; Fat 4.97g; Sodium 138mg; Carbs 49.62g; Fibre 5.8g; Sugar 28.47g; Protein 8.33g

# Whole-Wheat Blueberry Breakfast Cobbler

**Prep Time: 5 minutes | Cook Time: 15 minutes | Serves: 4**

40 g whole-wheat pastry flour
¾ teaspoon baking powder
Dash sea salt
120 ml low fat milk
2 tablespoons pure maple syrup

½ teaspoon vanilla extract
Cooking oil spray
75 g fresh blueberries
30 g plain store-bought granola

1. Whisk the flour, baking powder, and salt in a medium bowl. Add the maple syrup, milk, and vanilla extract, and gently whisk, just until thoroughly combined. 2. Preheat the unit by selecting BAKE, setting the temperature to 175°C, and setting the time to 3 minutes. Select START/STOP to begin. 3. Spray a 15-by-5-cm round baking pan with cooking oil and pour the batter into the pan. Top evenly with the blueberries and granola. 4. Once the unit is preheated, place the pan into the basket. 5. Select BAKE, set the temperature to 175°C, and set the time to 15 minutes. Select START/STOP to begin. 6. When the cooking is complete, the cobbler should be nicely browned and a knife inserted into the middle should come out clean. Enjoy plain or topped with a little vanilla yogurt.

**Per Serving:** Calories 109; Fat 1.36g; Sodium 55mg; Carbs 22.86g; Fibre 1.6g; Sugar 14.24g; Protein 2.48g

# Crispy French Toast Sticks

**Prep time: 10 minutes | Cook time: 9 minutes | Serves: 4**

2 eggs, beaten
180 ml milk
½ teaspoon vanilla extract
½ teaspoon ground cinnamon

65 g crushed crunchy cinnamon cereal, or any cereal flakes
4 slices toast
Maple syrup, for serving
Vegetable oil or melted butter

1. Combine the eggs, milk, vanilla and cinnamon in a bowl. Place the crushed cereal in another bowl. 2. Trim the crusts off the bread and cut each slice into 3 sticks. Dip the sticks of bread into the egg mixture. Roll the bread sticks in the cereal crumbs. 3. Pre-heat the air fryer to 205°C at "AIR FRY" mode for 5 minutes. Press START/STOP to begin preheating. 4. Spray the air fryer basket with oil. Place the coated sticks in the basket. 5. Air-fry the toast for 9 minutes. Turn the sticks over for even cooking. Serve warm with the maple syrup or some berries.
**Per Serving:** Calories 265; Fat 6.9g; Sodium 78mg; Carbs 55g; Fibre 25g; Sugar 16g; Protein 8g

# Crunch Bacon Veggie Bread Pudding

**Prep time: 8 minutes | Cook time: 52 minutes | Serves: 4**

225 g thick cut bacon, cut into ½ cm pieces
685 g brioche bread or rolls, cut into 1 cm cubes
3 eggs
240 ml milk

½ teaspoon salt
freshly ground black pepper
90 g frozen broccoli florets, thawed and chopped
150 g grated Swiss cheese

1. Pre-heat the air fryer to 205°C at "AIR FRY" mode for 5 minutes. Press START/STOP to begin preheating. 2. Air-fry the bacon for 6 to 10 minutes until crispy, shaking the basket a few times. Remove the bacon and set it aside on a paper towel. 3. Air-fry the brioche bread cubes for 2 minutes to dry and toast lightly. 4. Butter a 15 cm or 18 cm cake pan. Combine all of the ingredients in a bowl and toss well. Transfer the mixture to the cake pan, cover with aluminum foil and refrigerate the bread pudding overnight, or for at least 8 hours. 5. Remove the cake pan from the refrigerator an hour. 6. Pre-heat the air fryer to 165°C at "AIR FRY" mode for 5 minutes. Press START/STOP to begin preheating. Transfer the covered cake pan, to the basket of the air fryer Air-fry for 20 minutes. Remove the foil and air-fry for an additional 20 minutes. If the top starts to brown a little before the custard has set, simply return the foil to the pan. The bread pudding has cooked through when a skewer inserted into the centre and comes out clean.
**Per Serving:** Calories 789; Fat 7.9g; Sodium 412mg; Carbs 2g; Fibre 69g; Sugar 47g; Protein 12g

# Delicious Pepperoni Pizza Bread

**Prep time: 13 minutes | Cook time: 15 minutes | Serves: 6**

18 cm round bread boule
240 g grated mozzarella cheese
1 tablespoon dried oregano

240 g pizza sauce
140 g mini pepperoni or pepperoni slices

1. Make 7 to 8 deep slices across the bread boule, leaving 2.5 cm of bread uncut at the bottom of every slice before you reach the cutting board. Turn the bread boule 30°C and make 7 to 8 similar slices perpendicular to the first slices to form squares in the bread. Again, make sure you don't cut all the way through the bread. 2. Combine the mozzarella cheese and oregano in a bowl. 3. Fill the slices in the bread with pizza sauce. Top the sauce with the mozzarella cheese mixture and then the pepperoni. Keep spreading the bread apart and stuffing the ingredients in. 4. Pre-heat the air fryer to 160°C at "AIR FRY" mode for 5 minutes. Press START/STOP to begin preheating. 5. Transfer the bread boule to the air fryer basket and air-fry for 13 to 15 minutes, making sure the top doesn't get too dark. 6. Carefully remove the bread from the basket with a spatula. Transfer it to a serving platter with more sauce to dip into if desired.
**Per Serving:** Calories 458; Fat 7.9g; Sodium 258mg; Carbs 8g; Fibre 64g; Sugar 14g; Protein 78g

# Country-Style Gravy

**Prep time: 15 minutes | Cook time: 20 minutes | Serves: 6**

115 g pork sausage, casings removed
1 tablespoon butter
2 tablespoons flour
480 ml whole milk

½ teaspoon salt
Freshly ground black pepper
1 teaspoon fresh thyme leaves

1. Pre-heat a saucepan over medium heat. Add and brown the sausage, crumbling it into small pieces as it cooks. Add the butter and flour, stirring well to combine. Continue to cook for 2 minutes, stirring often. 2. Slowly pour in the milk, mixing as you do, and bring the mixture to a boil to thicken. Spice with salt and freshly ground black pepper. Place the sauce in the pan that fit in air fryer. Pre-heat the air fryer to 205°C at "AIR FRY" mode for 5 minutes. Press START/STOP to begin preheating. Cook the sauce for 3-5 minutes until thickened to desired consistency. Stir in the fresh thyme and serve hot.
**Per Serving:** Calories 789; Fat 7.9g; Sodium 412mg; Carbs 2g; Fibre 69g; Sugar 47g; Protein 12g

# Delicious Breakfast Toast

**Prep time: 3 minutes | Cook time: 7 minutes | Serves: 1**

1 strip of bacon, diced
1 slice of 2.5 cm thick bread
1 tablespoon softened butter

1 egg
salt and freshly ground black pepper
25 g grated Colby or Jack cheese

1. Pre-heat the air fryer to 205°C at "AIR FRY" mode for 5 minutes. Press START/STOP to begin preheating. 2. Air-fry the bacon for 3 minutes, shaking the basket once or twice while it cooks. Remove the bacon to a paper towel lined plate and set aside. 3. Score a large circle in the middle of the slice of bread, cutting halfway through, but not all the way through to the cutting board. Press down on the circle in the centre of the bread slice to create an indentation. If using, spread the softened butter on the edges and in the hole of the bread. 4. Transfer the slice of bread, hole side up, to the air fryer basket. Crack an egg into the centre of the bread, and spice with salt and pepper. 5. Pre-heat the air fryer to 195°C at "AIR FRY" mode for 5 minutes. Press START/STOP to begin preheating. Air-fry at 195°C for 5 minutes. Spread the grated cheese around the edges of the bread. Leaving the centre of the yolk uncovered, and top with the cooked bacon. Press the cheese and bacon into the bread lightly to help anchor it to the bread and prevent it from blowing around in the air fryer. 6. Air-fry for one or two more minutes just to melt the cheese and finish cooking the egg. Serve immediately.
**Per Serving:** Calories 254; Fat 7.9g; Sodium 2544mg; Carbs 2g; Fibre 10g; Sugar 6g; Protein 11g

# Cooked Eggs with Nutty Kale Pesto & Olives

**Prep time: 15 minutes | Cook time: 12 minutes | Serves: 2**

30 g roughly chopped kale leaves, stems and centre ribs removed
60 ml olive oil
25 g grated pecorino cheese
3 tablespoons whole almonds
1 garlic clove, peeled

Salt and freshly ground black pepper
4 large eggs
2 tablespoons heavy cream
3 tablespoons chopped pitted mixed olives
Toast, for serving

1. Pre-heat the air fryer to 150°C at "AIR FRY" mode for 5 minutes. Press START/STOP to begin preheating. 2. In a small blender, puree the kale, olive oil, pecorino, almonds, garlic, and salt and pepper until smooth. 3. Crack the eggs into a cake pan, then spoon the kale pesto over the egg whites only, leaving the yolks exposed. 4. Drizzle the cream over the yolks and swirl into the pesto. Place the pan in air fryer basket and cook until the eggs are just set and browned on top, 10 to 12 minutes. 5. Spread the olives over the eggs and serve hot with toast.
**Per Serving:** Calories 789; Fat 7.9g; Sodium 412mg; Carbs 2g; Fibre 69g; Sugar 47g; Protein 12g

# Cheesy Butternut Squash Frittata

**Prep time: 15 minutes | Cook time: 35 minutes | Serves: 3**

125 g cubed (1 cm) butternut squash
2 tablespoons olive oil
Salt and freshly ground black pepper
4 fresh sage leaves, thinly sliced

6 large eggs, lightly beaten
120 g ricotta cheese
Cayenne pepper

1. Pre-heat the air fryer to 205°C at "AIR FRY" mode for 5 minutes. Press START/STOP to begin preheating. 2. In a bowl, toss the squash with the olive oil and Spice with salt and black pepper until evenly coated. 3. Spread the sage on the bottom of a cake pan and place the squash on top. Place the pan in the air fryer and cook for 10 minutes. 4. Stir to incorporate the sage, then cook until the squash is tender and caramelized at the edges, about 3 minutes more. 5. Pour the eggs over the squash, dollop the ricotta all over, and spread with cayenne. 6. Reduce the temperature and Cook at 150°C until the eggs are set and the frittata is golden brown on top, about 20 minutes. 7. Remove the pan from the air fryer and cut the frittata into wedges to serve.
**Per Serving:** Calories 789; Fat 7.9g; Sodium 412mg; Carbs 2g; Fibre 69g; Sugar 47g; Protein 12g

# Breakfast Burritos

**Prep time: 15 minutes | Cook time: 10 minutes | Serves: 2**

2 large (25 cm to 30 cm) flour tortillas
130 g canned refried beans (pinto or black work equally well)
4 large eggs, cooked scrambled
4 corn tortilla chips, crushed

50 g grated pepper jack cheese
12 pickled jalapeño slices
1 tablespoon vegetable oil
Guacamole, salsa, and sour cream, for serving

1. Pre-heat the air fryer to 175°C at "AIR FRY" mode for 5 minutes. Press START/STOP to begin preheating. 2. Place the tortillas on sheet pan and divide the refried beans between them. 3. Top the beans with the scrambled eggs, crushed chips, pepper jack, and jalapeños. Fold one side over the fillings, like a burrito. 4. Brush the outside of the burritos with the oil, then transfer to the air fryer, seam-side down. 5. Cook until the tortillas are browned and crisp and the filling is warm throughout, about 10 minutes. 6. Transfer the chimichangas to plates and serve warm with guacamole, salsa, and sour cream, if you like.
**Per Serving:** Calories 254; Fat 7.9g; Sodium 2544mg; Carbs 2g; Fibre 10g; Sugar 6g; Protein 11g

# Cheese Veggie Frittata with Avocado Dressing

**Prep time: 15 minutes | Cook time: 15 minutes | Serves: 3**

75 g cherry tomatoes, halved
Salt
165 g fresh or thawed frozen corn kernels
60 ml milk
1 tablespoon finely chopped fresh dill
6 large eggs, lightly beaten
Freshly ground black pepper

50 g grated Monterey Jack cheese
1 avocado, pitted and peeled
2 tablespoons fresh lime juice
60 ml olive oil
8 fresh basil leaves, finely chopped
1 spring onion, finely chopped

1. Pre-heat the air fryer to 150°C at "AIR FRY" mode for 5 minutes. Press START/STOP to begin preheating. 2. Place the tomatoes in a colander and spread liberally with salt. Let stand for 10 minutes to drain off their excess moisture. 3. Transfer the tomatoes to a bowl and stir in the corn, milk, dill, and eggs. Spice with salt and pepper and mix to combine. 4. Pour the egg mixture into a cake pan and place the pan in the air fryer. Cook for 15 minutes, then spread with the Monterey Jack and until the cheese has melted and the eggs are set, 5 minutes more. 5. While the frittata cooks, in a bowl, mash the avocado with the lime juice until smooth, then stir in the olive oil, basil, and spring onion . 6. Remove the pan from the air fryer, cut the frittata into wedges, and serve with some of the avocado dressing.
**Per Serving:** Calories 458; Fat 7.9g; Sodium 258mg; Carbs 8g; Fibre 64g; Sugar 14g; Protein 78g

# Coconut Omelet with Nutmeg

**Prep time: 10 minutes | Cook time: 20 minutes | Serves:4**

Beaten 6 eggs
1 teaspoon. powdered nutmeg
25g Parmesan

½ teaspoon. coconut oil
60g coconut cream

1. Grate the Parmesan and combine it with the eggs, coconut cream, coconut oil, and nutmeg. 2. Add the liquid to the omelette in the air fryer basket, and cook it at 180°C for 20 minutes.
**Per Serving:** Calories 278; Fat 20.7g; Sodium 236mg; Carbs 5.63g; Fibre 0.4g; Sugar 1.1g; Protein 16.8g

# Quick Mascarpone Omelet

**Prep time:8 minutes | Cook time: 10 minutes | Serves:6**

8 beaten eggs
60g mascarpone

1 teaspoon black pepper
½ teaspoon coconut oil

1. Combine eggs, mascarpone, and freshly ground pepper. 2. Next, use coconut oil to lubricate the air fryer basket. 3. Include the egg mixture, and then cook the omelet at 195°C for 10 minutes.
**Per Serving:** Calories 180; Fat 13.2g; Sodium 137mg; Carbs 2.06g; Fibre 0.1g; Sugar 1.25g; Protein 12.11g

# Baked Cheese Chicken

**Prep time:5 minutes | Cook time: 25 minutes | Serves:4**

1 egg, beaten
30g shredded Mozzarella
140g chicken mince

1 teaspoon Italian seasonings
1 teaspoon coconut oil

1. Combine all the ingredients in a mixing dish and stir till just well combined. 2. After that, place it in the air fryer basket and cook for 25 minutes at 185°C .
**Per Serving:** Calories 1202; Fat 107.2g; Sodium 1994mg; Carbs 49.65g; Fibre 18.1g; Sugar 11.7g; Protein 17.13g

# Raisin Granola Bars

**Prep Time: 5 minutes | Cook Time: 15 minutes | Serves: 6**

Oil, for spraying
120g gluten-free rolled oats, divided
50g packed light brown sugar
1 teaspoon ground cinnamon
8 tablespoons unsalted butter, melted

3 tablespoons honey
1 tablespoon vegetable oil
1 teaspoon vanilla extract
2 tablespoons raisins

1. Line the baking pan with parchment paper and spray lightly with oil. 2. In a blender, Pulse about half of the oats until smooth in the blender, and then transfer to a medium bowl. 3. Add the remaining oats, brown sugar, and cinnamon and stir to combine; add the butter, honey, vegetable oil, and vanilla and stir to combine. Fold in the raisins. 4. Transfer the mixture to the baking pan, and press into an even layer. 5. Cook the mixture at 160°C for 10 minutes; when the time is up, increase the heat to 180°C and cook for 5 minutes more. 6. When cooked, let the dish cool to room temperature, and then freeze before cutting into bars and serving.
**Per Serving:** Calories 202; Fat 14.15g; Sodium 11mg; Carbs 22.8g; Fibre 3.3g; Sugar 9.29g; Protein 4.17g

# Pork Lettuce Wraps

### Prep time: 10 minutes | Cook time: 15 minutes | Serves:2

1 jalapeño pepper, minced
1 teaspoon coconut oil
1 teaspoon plain yogurt

½ teaspoon dried oregano
4 lettuce leaves
90g pork mince

1. Combine the pork mince with the oregano and jalapeño pepper. 2. Next, preheat the air fryer to 185°C. 3. Add the pork mince mixture and coconut oil. Cook the mixture for 15 minutes. Periodically give it a stir. 4. After that, transfer the pork mince mixture onto the lettuce leaves. Wrap the lettuce leaves and add plain yogurt.
**Per Serving:** Calories 325; Fat 23.18g; Sodium 77mg; Carbs 1.65g; Fibre 0.7g; Sugar 1.01g; Protein 26.13g

# Baked Avocado Egg Boat

### Prep time: 10 minutes | Cook time: 20 minutes | Serves:2

1 pitted and split avocado
2 eggs

25g grated Parmesan
½ teaspoon nutmeg

1. Break the eggs into the avocado hole, then sprinkle the cheese and crushed nutmeg on top. 2. After that, cook the avocado in the air fryer basket for 20 minutes at 190°C.
**Per Serving:** Calories 346; Fat 25.28g; Sodium 273mg; Carbs 15.54g; Fibre 6.8g; Sugar 1.54g; Protein 16.69g

# Cinnamon Bagels

### Prep Time: 30 minutes | Cook Time: 10 minutes | Serves: 4

Oil, for spraying
35g raisins
125g self-rising flour, plus more for dusting

240g plain Greek yogurt
1 teaspoon ground cinnamon
1 large egg

1. Line the air fryer basket with parchment and spray lightly with oil. 2. Place the raisins in a bowl of hot water, and let sit for 10 to 15 minutes, until they have plumped. This will make them extra juicy. 3. In a large bowl, Mix the flour, yogurt, and cinnamon in a large bowl until a ball is formed. 4. Drain the raisins and gently work them into the ball of dough. 5. Flour the work surface and place the dough on it. Roll each piece into an 20 or 23-cm-long rope, and shape it into a circle, pinching the ends together to seal. 6. Beat the egg in a bowl, and brush the egg onto the tops of the dough. 7. Place the dough in the prepared basket. 8. Cook the dough at 175°C for 10 minutes. 9. Serve warm.
**Per Serving:** Calories 163; Fat 3.43g; Sodium 403mg; Carbs 26.74g; Fibre 1.2g; Sugar 2.98g; Protein 5.92g

# Hard Eggs

### Prep Time: 5 minutes | Cook Time: 15 minutes | Serves: 6

Oil, for spraying

6 large eggs

1. Preheat the air fryer to 130°C. 2. Line the air fryer basket with parchment and spray lightly with oil. 2. Place the eggs in the air fryer basket. 3. Cook the eggs for 15 minutes. 4. Fill a bowl with water and ice, and then transfer the cooked eggs to the bowl; let the eggs sit for 1 minute or until cool enough to handle. 5. Use the paper towel to pat the eggs dry, and serve immediately. 6. You can refrigerate the cooked eggs for up to 7 days.
**Per Serving:** Calories 72; Fat 4.76g; Sodium 71mg; Carbs 0.36g; Fibre 0g; Sugar 0.19g; Protein 6.28g

# Sausage and Onion Patties

**Prep time: 10 minutes | Cook time: 20 minutes | Serves: 4**

300g pork sausage
1 tablespoon peeled and grated yellow onion
1 teaspoon dried thyme
⅛ teaspoon ground cumin

⅛ teaspoon red pepper flakes
¼ teaspoon salt
¼ teaspoon freshly ground black pepper
1 tablespoon water

1. Preheat air fryer at 175°C for 3 minutes. 2. Combine sausage, onion, thyme, cumin, red pepper flakes, salt, and black pepper in a large bowl. Form into eight patties. 3. Pour water into bottom of air fryer to ensure minimum smoke from fat drippings. Place 4 patties in air fryer basket lightly greased with olive oil and cook 5 minutes. 4. Flip patties and cook an additional 5 minutes. 5. Transfer patties to a large serving plate and repeat cooking with remaining sausage patties. Serve warm.
**Per Serving:** Calories 181; Fat 9g; Sodium 193mg; Carbs 0.7g; Fibre 0.2g; Sugar 0.2g; Protein 21.9g

# Scrambled Eggs

**Prep Time: 5 minutes | Cook Time: 10 minutes | Serves: 2**

1 teaspoon unsalted butter
2 large eggs
2 tablespoons milk

2 tablespoons shredded cheddar cheese
Salt
Freshly ground black pepper

1. Place the butter in the baking pan and cook in the air fryer at 150°C for 1 to 2 minutes until melted. 2. In a small bowl, Beat the eggs with milk, and cheese in a bowl, and season with salt and black pepper. Transfer the mixture to the baking pan. 3. Cook them for 3 minutes. Stir the eggs and push them toward the centre of the pan. 4. Cook for another 2 minutes, then stir again. 5. Cook for another 2 minutes, until the eggs are just cooked. 6. Serve warm.
**Per Serving:** Calories 88; Fat 6.93g; Sodium 171mg; Carbs 2.12g; Fibre 0g; Sugar 1.35g; Protein 4.2g

# Grilled Grapefruit with Cinnamon

**Prep time: 5 minutes | Cook time: 4 minutes | Serves: 2**

1 large grapefruit, cut in half
1 tablespoon granular erythritol
2 teaspoons ground cinnamon

⅛ teaspoon ground ginger
2 teaspoons butter, divided into 2 pats

1. Preheat air fryer at 205°C for 3 minutes. 2. Using a paring knife, cut each grapefruit section away from the inner membrane, keeping the sections remaining in the fruit. 3. In a small bowl, combine erythritol, cinnamon, and ginger. Sprinkle over tops of grapefruit halves. Place 1 pat butter on top of each half. 4. Place grapefruit halves in ungreased air fryer basket and cook 4 minutes. 5. Transfer to a medium serving plate and serve warm.
**Per Serving:** Calories 118; Fat 4g; Sodium 31mg; Carbs 21.8g; Fibre 3.2g; Sugar 17.9g; Protein 1.2g

# Air-Fried Eggs

**Prep time: 5 minutes | Cook time: 15 minutes | Serves: 8**

8 large eggs
240g ice cubes

480g water

1. Preheat air fryer at 120°C for 3 minutes. 2. Add eggs to ungreased air fryer basket. Cook for 15 minutes. 3. Add the ice cubes and water to a large bowl. Transfer cooked eggs to this water bath immediately to stop cooking process. After 5 minutes, peel eggs and serve.
**Per Serving:** Calories 72; Fat 4.7g; Sodium 72mg; Carbs 0.4g; Fibre 0g; Sugar 0.2g; Protein 6.3g

# Sausage-Cheese Balls

**Prep time: 10 minutes | Cook time: 12 minutes | Serves: 4**

115g loose chorizo
340g pork sausage meat
2 tablespoons canned green chilies, including juice

25g cream cheese, room temperature
25g shredded sharp Cheddar cheese

1. Before cooking, heat your air fryer to 205°C, for about 3 minutes. 2. In a large bowl, combine all ingredients. Form mixture into sixteen 2.5 cm balls. Place sausage balls in ungreased air fryer basket. 3. Cook for 6 minutes, then shake basket and cook an additional 6 minutes until a meat thermometer ensures an internal temperature of at least 60°C . 4. Transfer to a large serving plate and serve warm.
**Per Serving:** Calories 456; Fat 38.5g; Sodium 1136mg; Carbs 2.3g; Fibre 0.1g; Sugar 1.2g; Protein 24.8g

# Banana-Nut Muffins

**Prep Time: 5 minutes | Cook Time: 15 minutes | Serves: 10**

Oil, for spraying
2 very ripe bananas
100g packed light brown sugar
80ml vegetable oil
1 large egg

1 teaspoon vanilla extract
90g plain flour
1 teaspoon baking powder
1 teaspoon ground cinnamon
60g chopped walnuts

1. Preheat the air fryer to 160°C. Spray 10 silicone muffin cups lightly with oil. 2. In a medium bowl, mash the bananas. 3. Add the brown sugar, oil, egg, and vanilla to the banana bowl, and stir to combine; fold in the flour, baking powder, and cinnamon; add the walnuts and fold a few times to distribute throughout the batter. 4. Divide the batter equally among the prepared muffin cups and place them in the basket. You can work in batches. 5. Cook the muffins in the preheated air fryer for 15 minutes, or until golden brown and a toothpick inserted into the centre of a muffin comes out clean. 6. Let the muffins cool on a wire rack before serving.
**Per Serving:** Calories 164; Fat 11.77g; Sodium 5mg; Carbs 13.36g; Fibre 1.2g; Sugar 2.76g; Protein 2.2g

# Maple Chicken and Waffles

**Prep time: 10 minutes | Cook time: 30 minutes | Serves: 4**

8 whole chicken wings
1 teaspoon garlic powder
Chicken seasoning, for preparing the chicken
Freshly ground black pepper

65g plain flour
Cooking oil spray
8 frozen waffles
Pure maple syrup, for serving (optional)

1. In a medium bowl, combine the chicken and garlic powder and season with chicken seasoning and pepper. Toss to coat. 2. Place the seasoned chicken to a resealable plastic bag and add the flour. Seal the bag and shake it to coat the chicken thoroughly. 3. Insert the crisper plate into the air fryer basket and then put the basket into the unit. 4. To preheat, set your air fryer on Air Fry mode and set the temperature to 205°C and time to 3 minutes. 5. Once the unit is preheated, spray the cooking oil over the crisper plate. Transfer the marinated chicken from the bag to the basket with tongs. It is okay to stack the chicken wings on top of each other. Spray them with cooking oil. 6. Set the air fryer on Air Fry mode at 205°C, and set the time to 20 minutes. 7. Remove the basket and shake the wings halfway after cooking for 5 minutes. Return the basket to resume cooking. Shake the basket every 5 minutes until the chicken is fully cooked. 8. When the cooking is complete, remove the cooked chicken from the basket; cover to keep warm. 9. Rinse the basket and crisper plate with warm water. Insert them back into the unit. 10. Set the air fryer on Air Fry mode, adjust the temperature setting to 180°C, and set the time to 3 minutes. Once the unit is preheated, spray the cooking oil over the crisper plate. Working in batches, place the frozen waffles into the basket. Do not stack them. Spray the waffles with cooking oil. 11. Set the air fryer on Air Fry mode, adjust the temperature setting to 180°C, and set the time to 6 minutes. When the cooking is complete, repeat the cooking steps with the remaining waffles. 12. Serve the waffles with the chicken and a touch of maple syrup, if desired.
**Per Serving:** Calories 338; Fat 9g; Sodium 638mg; Carbs 43.7g; Fibre 2.3g; Sugar 3.7g; Protein 19g

# Air Fried Bacon Strips

**Prep time: 5 minutes | Cook time: 12 minutes | Serves: 4**

2 tablespoons water

8 slices bacon, halved

1. Before cooking, heat your air fryer to 205°C, for about 3 minutes. 2. Pour water into bottom of air fryer to ensure minimum smoke from fat drippings. Place half of bacon in ungreased air fryer basket and cook for 3 minutes. Flip, then cook an additional 3 minutes. 3. Transfer cooked bacon to a medium paper towel–lined serving plate and repeat cooking with remaining bacon. Serve warm.
**Per Serving:** Calories 212; Fat 20.4g; Sodium 245mg; Carbs 0.4g; Fibre 0g; Sugar 0.4g; Protein 6.5g

# Vegetable Bacon Hash

**Prep time: 10 minutes | Cook time: 12 minutes | Serves: 4**

25 small Brussels sprouts, halved
2 mini sweet peppers, seeded and diced
1 small yellow onion, peeled and diced
3 slices bacon, diced

2 tablespoons fresh orange juice
¼ teaspoon salt
1 teaspoon orange zest

1. Before cooking, heat your air fryer to 175°C, for about 3 minutes. 2. In a medium bowl, combine all ingredients except orange zest. 3. Add mixture to ungreased air fryer basket. Cook for 6 minutes, then toss and cook an additional 6 minutes. Serve warm.
**Per Serving:** Calories 154; Fat 8g; Sodium 268mg; Carbs 16.4g; Fibre 5.3g; Sugar 4g; Protein 7.2g

# Scrambled Eggs with Cheese

**Prep time: 5 minutes | Cook time: 7 minutes | Serves: 2**

4 large eggs
¼ teaspoon salt
⅛ teaspoon freshly ground black pepper

2 teaspoons sour cream
1 tablespoon goat cheese crumbles
1 tablespoon chopped fresh parsley, divided

1. Before cooking, heat your air fryer to 205°C, for about 3 minutes. 2. In a small bowl, whisk together eggs, salt, and pepper. 3. Add egg mixture to a cake tin lightly greased with olive oil. Add barrel to air fryer basket and cook for 5 minutes. 4. Remove cake tin from air fryer and use a silicone spatula to stir eggs. Add sour cream, goat cheese, and half of parsley. Place barrel back in the air fryer and cook an additional 2 minutes. 5. Transfer eggs to a medium serving dish and garnish with remaining parsley. Serve warm.
**Per Serving:** Calories 370; Fat 29.8g; Sodium 614mg; Carbs 2.3g; Fibre 0.1g; Sugar 1g; Protein 22g

# Maple Sage Links

**Prep time: 10 minutes | Cook time: 9 minutes | Serves: 8**

300g mild pork sausage meat, loosen or removed from casings
1 teaspoon rubbed sage
2 tablespoons pure maple syrup

⅛ teaspoon cayenne pepper
¼ teaspoon salt
¼ teaspoon freshly ground black pepper
1 tablespoon water

1. Before cooking, heat your air fryer to 205°C, for about 3 minutes. 2. Combine pork, sage, maple syrup, cayenne pepper, salt, and black pepper. Form into eight links. 3. Pour water into bottom of air fryer. Place links in air fryer basket. Cook for 9 minutes. 4. Transfer to a plate and serve warm.
**Per Serving:** Calories 265; Fat 26g; Sodium 339mg; Carbs 3.5g; Fibre 0.1g; Sugar 3g; Protein 3.3g

# Shakshuka Cups

**Prep time: 10 minutes | Cook time: 22 minutes | Serves: 4**

1 tablespoon olive oil
½ medium yellow onion, peeled and diced
2 cloves garlic, peeled and minced
1 (1-cm) knob turmeric, peeled and minced
1 (360g) can diced tomatoes, including juice
1 tablespoon no-sugar-added tomato paste
½ teaspoon smoked paprika
½ teaspoon salt

½ teaspoon granular erythritol
¼ teaspoon ground cumin
¼ teaspoon ground coriander
⅛ teaspoon cayenne pepper
4 small peppers, any colour, tops removed and seeded
4 large eggs
2 tablespoons feta cheese crumbles
2 tablespoons chopped fresh parsley

1. Set a suitable saucepan over medium heat and then add olive oil to heat for 30 seconds. Add onion and stir-fry for 10 minutes until softened. 2. Add garlic and turmeric to pan and heat another minute. Add diced tomatoes, tomato paste, paprika, salt, erythritol, cumin, coriander, and cayenne pepper. Remove from heat and stir. 3. Before cooking, heat your air fryer to 175°C, for about 3 minutes. 4. Place peppers in ungreased air fryer basket. Divide tomato mixture among peppers. Crack one egg onto tomato mixture in each pepper. 5. Cook for 9 minutes, then remove from air fryer and sprinkle feta cheese on top of eggs. Then return in air fryer and cook for 1 minute. 6. Remove from air fryer and let rest 5 minutes on a large serving plate. Garnish with parsley and serve warm.
**Per Serving:** Calories 341; Fat 24g; Sodium 1172mg; Carbs 14.8g; Fibre 3.4g; Sugar 9.6g; Protein 18.4g

# Pumpkin and Walnut Muffins

**Prep time: 10 minutes | Cook time: 7 minutes | Serves: 6**

50g almond flour
15g granular erythritol
½ teaspoon baking powder
¼ teaspoon pumpkin pie spice
⅛ teaspoon ground nutmeg
⅛ teaspoon salt

60g pumpkin purée
¼ teaspoon vanilla extract
3 tablespoons butter, melted
2 large eggs
30g crushed walnuts

1. Before cooking, heat your air fryer to 190°C, for about 3 minutes. 2. In a large bowl, combine flour, erythritol, baking powder, pumpkin pie spice, nutmeg, and salt. Set aside. 3. In a medium bowl, combine pumpkin purée, vanilla, butter, and eggs. Pour wet ingredients into bowl with dry ingredients and gently combine. 4. Add walnuts to batter. Do not overmix. Spoon batter into six silicone cupcake liners lightly greased with olive oil. 5. Place cupcake liners in the air fryer basket and cook for 7 minutes. 6. Transfer muffins in silicone liners to a cooling rack to cool for 5 minutes, then serve.
**Per Serving:** Calories 193; Fat 12g; Sodium 134mg; Carbs 17g; Fibre 1.6g; Sugar 8.4g; Protein 5.5g

# Savoury Puffed Egg Tarts

**Prep time: 10 minutes | Cook time: 17 to 20 minutes | Serves: 2**

⅓ sheet frozen puff pastry, thawed
Cooking oil spray
50g shredded Cheddar cheese

2 eggs
¼ teaspoon salt, divided
1 teaspoon minced fresh parsley (optional)

1. Insert the crisper plate into the basket of your air fryer. 2. To preheat, set your air fryer on Bake mode and set the temperature to 200°C and time to 3 minutes. 3. Lay the puff pastry sheet on a piece of parchment paper and cut it in half. 4. Once the unit is preheated, spray the crisper plate with cooking oil. Transfer the 2 squares of pastry to the basket, keeping them on the parchment paper. 5. Select BAKE, set the temperature to 200°C, and set the time to 20 minutes. 6. After 10 minutes, use a metal spoon to press down the centre of each pastry square to make a well. Divide the cheese equally between the baked pastries. On top of the cheese, carefully crack an egg, and sprinkle each with the salt. Resume cooking for 7 to 10 minutes. 7. When the cooking is complete, the eggs will be cooked through. Sprinkle each with parsley (if using) and serve.
**Per Serving:** Calories 404; Fat 29.4g; Sodium 638mg; Carbs 19g; Fibre 0.6g; Sugar 0.6g; Protein 15g

# Vanilla Strawberry Muffins

**Prep time: 10 minutes | Cook time: 7 minutes | Serves: 6**

50g almond flour
15g granular erythritol
½ teaspoon baking powder
⅛ teaspoon salt
75g hulled and finely chopped fresh strawberries

¼ teaspoon vanilla extract
3 tablespoons butter, melted
2 large eggs
1 tablespoon chopped fresh basil

1. Before cooking, heat your air fryer to 190°C, for about 3 minutes. 2. In a large bowl, combine almond flour, erythritol, baking powder, and salt. Set aside. 3. In a medium bowl, combine strawberries, vanilla, butter, and eggs. Pour wet ingredients into large bowl with dry ingredients. Gently combine. 4. Add basil to batter. Do not overmix. Spoon batter into six silicone cupcake liners lightly greased with olive oil. 5. Place liners in air fryer basket and cook for 7 minutes. 6. Transfer muffins in silicone liners to a cooling rack to cool for 5 minutes, then serve.
**Per Serving:** Calories 145; Fat 8.2g; Sodium 122mg; Carbs 14.6g; Fibre 1.2g; Sugar 1g; Protein 4g

# Paprika Hash Browns

**Prep time: 15 minutes | Cook time: 20 minutes | Serves: 4**

4 russet potatoes, peeled
1 teaspoon paprika
Salt

Freshly ground black pepper
Cooking oil spray

1. Shred the peeled russet potatoes with a box grater or food processor. If your grater has different hole sizes, use the largest holes. 2. Place the potatoes in a suitable bowl of cold water. Let sit for 5 minutes. (Cold water helps remove excess starch from the potatoes.) Stir them to help dissolve the starch. 3. Insert the crisper plate into the basket of your air fryer. To preheat, set your air fryer on Air Fry mode and set the temperature to 180°C and time to 3 minutes. 4. Drain and pat them with paper towels until the potatoes are completely dry. Season the potatoes with the paprika, salt, and pepper. 5. Once it is preheated, spray the crisper plate with cooking oil. Spray the potatoes with the cooking oil and place them into the basket. 6. Select AIR FRY, set the temperature to 180°C, and set the time to 20 minutes. Remove the basket and shake the potatoes halfway after cooking for 5 minutes. Reinsert the basket to resume cooking. Continue shaking the basket every 5 minutes (a total of 4 times) until the potatoes are done. 7. When the cooking is complete, remove the hash browns from the basket and serve warm.
**Per Serving:** Calories 293; Fat 0.4g; Sodium 19mg; Carbs 67g; Fibre 5g; Sugar 2.4g; Protein 8g

# Classic Dijon Scotch Eggs

**Prep time: 10 minutes | Cook time: 14 minutes | Serves: 4**

455g pork sausage
2 teaspoons Dijon mustard
2 teaspoons peeled and grated yellow onion
1 tablespoon chopped fresh chives
1 tablespoon chopped fresh parsley
⅛ teaspoon ground nutmeg

½ teaspoon salt
¼ teaspoon freshly ground black pepper
4 large hard-boiled eggs, peeled
1 large egg, beaten
100g parmesan, grated
2 teaspoons olive oil

1. Before cooking, heat your air fryer to 175°C, for about 3 minutes. 2. Combine sausage, mustard, onion, chives, parsley, nutmeg, salt, and pepper in a large bowl. Separate mixture into four even balls. 3. Form sausage balls evenly around hard-boiled eggs, then dip in beaten egg and dredge in parmesan. 4. Place sausage balls in air fryer basket lightly greased with olive oil. Cook 7 minutes, then gently turn and brush lightly with olive oil. Cook an additional 7 minutes. 5. Transfer to a suitable serving plate and serve warm.
**Per Serving:** Calories 481; Fat 32.8g; Sodium 1406mg; Carbs 16.7g; Fibre 1.7g; Sugar 9g; Protein 29g

# Chapter 2 Vegetable and Side Recipes

# Delicious Roasted Carrots

**Prep Time: 5 minutes | Cook Time: 12 minutes | Serves: 4**

455 g baby carrots
2 tablespoons dry ranch seasoning

3 tablespoons salted butter, melted

1. Preheat the air fryer to 180°C. 2. Put carrots into a 15 cm round baking dish. Sprinkle carrots with ranch seasoning and drizzle with butter. Gently toss to coat. 3. Put in the air fryer basket and cook them for 12 minutes, stirring twice during cooking, until carrots are tender.
**Per Serving:** Calories 104; Fat 5.92g; Sodium 420mg; Carbs 11.81g; Fibre 4g; Sugar 4.38g; Protein 1.11g

# Flavourful Sweet Roasted Carrots

**Prep Time: 5 minutes | Cook Time: 12 minutes | Serves: 4**

455 g baby carrots
55 g brown sugar
2 tablespoons salted butter, melted

¼ teaspoon garlic powder
½ teaspoon salt
¼ teaspoon ground black pepper

1. Preheat the air fryer to 180°C. 2. Put carrots into a 15 cm round baking dish. 3. Mix brown sugar, butter, and garlic powder. Pour mixture over carrots and carefully stir to coat. Sprinkle with salt and pepper. 4. Put in the air fryer basket and cook them for 12 minutes, stirring three times during cooking, until carrots are tender.
**Per Serving:** Calories 127; Fat 4.02g; Sodium 853mg; Carbs 23.22g; Fibre 3.5g; Sugar 17.4g; Protein 1.01g

# Sweet Brussels Sprouts

**Prep Time: 5 minutes | Cook Time: 15 minutes | Serves: 4**

455 g Brussels Sprouts, trimmed and halved
2 tablespoons olive oil

½ teaspoon salt
¼ teaspoon ground black pepper

1. Preheat the air fryer to 175°C. 2. In a container, put Brussels sprouts and drizzle with oil. Sprinkle with salt and pepper. 3. Put in the air fryer basket and cook 15 minutes, shaking the air fryer basket three times during cooking. 4. Serve warm.
**Per Serving:** Calories 110; Fat 7.1g; Sodium 853mg; Carbs 10.42g; Fibre 4.4g; Sugar 2.64g; Protein 3.89g

# Golden and Crispy Potato Balls

**Prep Time: 15 minutes | Cook Time: 10 minutes | Serves: 4**

460 g mashed potatoes (about 4 medium russet potatoes)
170 g sour cream, divided
1 teaspoon salt
½ teaspoon ground black pepper

100 g shredded sharp Cheddar cheese
4 slices bacon, cooked and crumbled
110 g panko bread crumbs

1. Preheat the air fryer to 205°C. Cut parchment paper to fit the air fryer basket. 2. In a container, mix mashed potatoes, 115 g sour cream, salt, pepper, Cheddar, and bacon. Form twelve balls using 2 tablespoons of the potato mixture per ball. 3. Divide remaining 55 g sour cream evenly among mashed potato balls, coating each before rolling in bread crumbs. 4. Put balls on parchment in the air fryer basket and spritz with cooking spray. Cook them for 10 minutes until brown. 5. Serve warm.
**Per Serving:** Calories 252; Fat 15.37g; Sodium 815mg; Carbs 21.5g; Fibre 2g; Sugar 13.12g; Protein 7.5g

# Lemon Butter Asparagus

**Prep Time: 5 minutes | Cook Time: 15 minutes | Serves: 4**

455 g asparagus, ends trimmed
55 g salted butter, cubed
Zest and juice of ½ medium lemon

½ teaspoon salt
¼ teaspoon ground black pepper

1. Preheat the air fryer to 190°C. Cut a 15 cm × 15 cm square of foil. 2. Put asparagus on foil square. 3. Dot asparagus with butter. Sprinkle lemon zest, salt, and pepper on top of asparagus. Drizzle lemon juice over asparagus. 4. Fold foil over asparagus and seal the edges closed to form a packet. 5. Put in the air fryer basket and cook them for 15 minutes until tender. 6. Serve them warm.

**Per Serving:** Calories 93; Fat 7.82g; Sodium 853mg; Carbs 5.09g; Fibre 2.4g; Sugar 2.43g; Protein 2.65g

# Classic Green Bean Casserole

**Prep Time: 10 minutes | Cook Time: 20 minutes | Serves: 4**

1 (250 g) can condensed cream of mushroom soup
60 g heavy cream
2 (360 g) cans cut green beans, drained
1 teaspoon minced garlic

½ teaspoon salt
¼ teaspoon ground black pepper
55 g packaged French fried onions

1. Preheat the air fryer to 160°C. 2. In a 4-litre baking dish, pour soup and cream over green beans and mix to combine. 3. Stir in garlic, salt, and pepper until combined. Top with French fried onions. 4. Put in the air fryer basket and cook for 20 minutes until top is lightly brown and dish is heated through. 5. Serve warm.

**Per Serving:** Calories 110; Fat 6.27g; Sodium 853mg; Carbs 12.84g; Fibre 3.3g; Sugar 3.97g; Protein 2.89g

# Roasted Yellow Beans with Tangy Tomatoes

**Prep time: 5 minutes | Cook time: 8 minutes | Serves: 3**

225 g yellow beans, trimmed
2 small Ingredients
tomatoes, sliced

1 tablespoon sesame oil
Sea salt and ground black pepper

1. Toss the green beans and tomatoes with the sesame oil, salt, and black pepper; toss until they are well coated. 2. Arrange the vegetables in the Air Fryer basket. Cook the green beans at 200°Cfor 8 minutes; make sure to stir your vegetables halfway through the cooking time. 3. Taste, adjust the seasonings,and serve immediately. Bon appétit!

**Per Serving:** Calories 254; Fat 7.9g; Sodium 2544mg; Carbs 2g; Fibre 10g; Sugar 6g; Protein 11g

# Delicious Roasted Cremini Mushrooms

**Prep time: 5 minutes | Cook time: 7 minutes | Serves: 4**

455 g cremini mushrooms, sliced
2 tablespoons olive oil
½ teaspoon shallot powder
½ teaspoon garlic powder

1 tablespoon coconut aminos
1 tablespoon white wine
Sea salt and ground black pepper,
1 tablespoon fresh parsley, chopped

1. Toss the mushrooms with the remaining ingredients. Toss until they are well coated on all sides. 2. Arrange the mushrooms in the Air Fryer basket. Cook your mushrooms at 205°C for about 7 minutes, shaking the basket halfway through the cooking time. 3. Garnish with the fresh herbs, if desired. Bon appétit!

**Per Serving:** Calories 458; Fat 7.9g; Sodium 258mg; Carbs 8g; Fibre 64g; Sugar 14g; Protein 78g

# Quick Yeast Rolls

**Prep Time: 10 minutes | Cook Time: 75 minutes | Serves: 16**

4 tablespoons salted butter
50 g granulated sugar
240 ml hot water
1 tablespoon quick-rise yeast

1 large egg
1 teaspoon salt
315 g flour, divided

1. In a microwave-safe bowl, microwave butter for 30 seconds until melted. Pour 2 tablespoons of butter into a container. Add sugar, hot water, and yeast. Mix until yeast is dissolved. 2. Using a rubber spatula, mix in egg, salt, and 280 g flour. Dough will be very sticky. 3. Cover bowl with plastic wrap and let rise in a warm put for 1 hour. 4. Sprinkle the remaining 30 g flour on dough and turn onto a lightly floured surface. Knead 2 minutes, then cut into sixteen even pieces. 5. Preheat the air fryer to 175°C. Spray a 15 cm round cake pan with cooking spray. 6. Sprinkle each roll with flour and arrange in pan. Brush with remaining melted butter. Put pan in the air fryer basket and cook them for 10 minutes until fluffy and golden on top. 7. Serve warm.
**Per Serving:** Calories 85; Fat 2.35g; Sodium 195mg; Carbs 13.75g; Fibre 0.5g; Sugar 13.12g; Protein 2.07g

# Great Southwest-Style Corn Cobs

**Prep Time: 5 minutes | Cook Time: 15 minutes | Serves: 6**

115 g sour cream
1½ teaspoons chili powder
Juice and zest of 1 medium lime

¼ teaspoon salt
6 mini corn cobs
120 g crumbled feta cheese

1. Preheat the air fryer to 175°C. 2. Mix sour cream, chili powder, lime zest and juice, and salt. 3. Brush mixture all over corn cobs and put them in the air fryer basket. Cook them for 15 minutes until corn is tender. 4. Sprinkle with cotija.
**Per Serving:** Calories 221; Fat 5.81g; Sodium 853mg; Carbs 41.28g; Fibre 4.8g; Sugar 0.43g; Protein 8.01g

# Delicious Garlic Bread

**Prep Time: 10 minutes | Cook Time: 12 minutes | Serves: 6**

130 g self-rising flour
245 g plain full-fat Greek yogurt
55 g salted butter, softened

1 tablespoon minced garlic
115 g shredded mozzarella cheese

1. Preheat the air fryer to 160°C. Cut parchment paper to fit the air fryer basket. 2. In a container, mix flour and yogurt until a sticky, soft dough forms. Let sit 5 minutes. 3. Turn dough onto a lightly floured surface. Knead dough 1 minute, then replace to prepared parchment. Press out into an 20 cm round. 4. Mix Butter and garlic. Brush over dough. Sprinkle with mozzarella. 5. Put in the air fryer and cook them for 12 minutes until edges are golden and cheese is brown.
**Per Serving:** Calories 173; Fat 5.95g; Sodium 459mg; Carbs 19.47g; Fibre 0.9g; Sugar 3.22g; Protein 10.32g

# Crispy Roasted Gold Potatoes

**Prep time: 10minutes | Cook time: 13 minutes | Serves: 3**

340 g Yukon Gold potatoes, peeled and cut into 2.5 cm chunks
1 tablespoon olive oil
Sea salt and ground black pepper,

½ turmeric powder
½ teaspoon garlic powder
½ teaspoon paprika

1. Toss the potatoes with the remaining ingredients until well coated on all sides. 2. Arrange the potatoes in the Air Fryer basket. Cook the potatoes at 205°C for about 13 minutes, shaking the basket halfway through the cooking time. Bon appétit!
**Per Serving:** Calories 789; Fat 7.9g; Sodium 412mg; Carbs 2g; Fibre 69g; Sugar 47g; Protein 12g

# Easy Caponata

**Prep time: 10minutes | Cook time: 10 minutes | Serves: 3**

3 peppers, sliced
1 medium-sized onion, sliced
2 tablespoons olive oil

50 g olives, pitted and sliced
1 large tomato, sliced
1 teaspoon capers, drained

1. Toss the peppers, onion, and olive oil in the Air Fryer cooking basket. 2. Cook the vegetables at 205°C for about 10 minutes, shaking the basket halfway through the cooking time. 3. Add in the olives, tomato, and capers. Continue to cook an additional 5 minutes or until everything is cooked through. Bon appétit!
**Per Serving:** Calories 254; Fat 7.9g; Sodium 2544mg; Carbs 2g; Fibre 10g; Sugar 6g; Protein 11g

# Cheesy Broccoli Florets

**Prep time: 4 minutes | Cook time: 6 minutes | Serves: 3**

340 g broccoli florets
1 tablespoon olive oil
½ teaspoon dried dill weed

Coarse sea salt and freshly ground black pepper, to taste
50 g parmesan cheese, freshly grated

1. Toss the broccoli florets with the olive oil, dill, salt, and black pepper until well coated. 2. Arrange the broccoli florets in the Air Fryer basket. Cook the broccoli florets at 200°C for 6 minutes, shaking the basket halfway through the cooking time. Top with the parmesan cheese and serve warm. Bon appétit!
**Per Serving:** Calories 458; Fat 7.9g; Sodium 258mg; Carbs 8g; Fibre 64g; Sugar 14g; Protein 78g

# Cauliflower Chickpeas Salad

**Prep time: 7 minutes | Cook time: 12 minutes | Serves: 4**

455 g cauliflower florets
260 g chickpeas, canned or boiled
60 g mayonnaise
1 teaspoon Dijon mustard

1 teaspoon ancho chili powder
Sea salt and ground black pepper,
2 tablespoons fresh chives, chopped
2 tablespoons apple cider vinegar

1. Arrange the cauliflower florets in a lightly greased Air Fryer basket. 2. Cook the cauliflower florets at 205°C for 12 minutes, shaking the basket halfway through the cooking time. 3. Thoroughly combine the cauliflower florets with the remaining ingredients. Serve well-chilled and enjoy!
**Per Serving:** Calories 789; Fat 7.9g; Sodium 412mg; Carbs 2g; Fibre 69g; Sugar 47g; Protein 12g

# Cheesy Beetroot

**Prep time: 22 minutes | Cook time: 40 minutes | Serves: 4**

455 g beetroot, whole
Sea salt and red pepper flakes,
2 tablespoons apple cider vinegar

4 tablespoons olive oil
1 teaspoon garlic powder
100 g feta cheese, crumbled

1. Arrange your beetroot in the Air Fryer basket. Cook the beats at 205°C for 40 minutes, shaking the basket halfway through the cooking time. 2. Let them cool completely. Peel the beetroot and cut them into thin slices; transfer to a salad bowl. 3. Add in the remaining ingredients and stir to combine. Bon appétit!
**Per Serving:** Calories 254; Fat 7.9g; Sodium 2544mg; Carbs 2g; Fibre 10g; Sugar 6g; Protein 11g

# Roasted Green Beans with Cheese and Pistachio

**Prep time: 5 minutes | Cook time: 7 minutes | Serves: 3**

340 g green beans, cleaned and trimmed
1 tablespoon olive oil
1 clove garlic, pressed

Sea salt and ground black pepper,
50 g feta cheese, crumbled
1 tablespoon pistachio, chopped

1. Toss the green beans with the olive oil, garlic, salt, and black pepper until they are well coated. Arrange the green beans in the Air Fryer basket. 2. Cook the green beans at 190°C for 7 minutes; make sure to check the green beans halfway through the cooking time. 3. Taste, adjust the seasonings, and serve garnished with cheese and chopped pistachio. Enjoy!
**Per Serving:** Calories 458; Fat 7.9g; Sodium 258mg; Carbs 8g; Fibre 64g; Sugar 14g; Protein 78g

# Chinese-Style Spiced Brussels Sprouts

**Prep time: 7 minutes | Cook time: 14 minutes | Serves: 2**

225 g Brussels sprouts, trimmed
2 tablespoons sesame oil
Sea salt and ground black pepper,

1 teaspoon Five-spice powder
1 teaspoon soy sauce
1 teaspoon rice vinegar

1. Toss the Brussels sprouts with the oil until well coated on all sides; then, arrange the Brussels sprouts in the Air Fryer basket. 2. Cook the Brussels sprouts at 195°C for 10 minutes, shaking the basket halfway through the cooking time. 3. Toss them with the remaining ingredients and continue to cook for 3 to 4 minutes more. Serve warm and enjoy!
**Per Serving:** Calories 789; Fat 7.9g; Sodium 412mg; Carbs 2g; Fibre 69g; Sugar 47g; Protein 12g

# Italian-Style Aubergine Fries

**Prep time: 7 minutes | Cook time: 13 minutes | Serves: 4**

2 eggs, mixed
50 g almond flour
50 g Parmesan cheese, grated

1 teaspoon Italian Spicing mix
340 g aubergine, peeled and sliced

1. In a mixing bowl, thoroughly combine the eggs, almond flour, cheese, and Italian spicing mix. 2. Dip the aubergine slices in the egg flour mixture until they are well coated on all sides. Arrange the aubergine in the Air Fryer basket. Cook the aubergine at 205°C for about 13 minutes, shaking the basket halfway through the cooking time. Bon appétit!
**Per Serving:** Calories 254; Fat 7.9g; Sodium 2544mg; Carbs 2g; Fibre 10g; Sugar 6g; Protein 11g

# Herbed Cauliflower

**Prep time: 7 minutes | Cook time: 13 minutes | Serves: 3**

340 g cauliflower florets
1 tablespoon olive oil
½ teaspoon dried oregano

1 teaspoon dried basil
1 teaspoon dried rosemary
Sea salt and ground black pepper

1. Toss the cauliflower florets and onion with the olive oil and spices. Toss until they are well coated on all sides. 2. Arrange the cauliflower florets in the Air Fryer basket. Cook the cauliflower florets at 205°C for about 13 minutes, shaking the basket halfway through the cooking time. Bon appétit!
**Per Serving:** Calories 458; Fat 7.9g; Sodium 258mg; Carbs 8g; Fibre 64g; Sugar 14g; Protein 78g

# Crispy Steak Fries with Toum

**Prep time: 10 minutes | Cook time: 25 minutes | Serves: 4**

910 g russet potatoes, cut into 1.3 cm fries
135 g garlic cloves, peeled
3 teaspoons salt, divided
5 to 6 tablespoons (75 to 90ml) freshly squeezed lemon

juice, chilled or iced, divided
600 ml rapeseed or other neutral oil, chilled, divided, plus 1 tablespoon (15ml)

1. Place the potato slices in a bowl and cover with cold water. Soak for at least 30 minutes and up to several hours to remove excess starch. 2. While the potatoes are soaking, make the toum. Place the garlic cloves in a food processor along with 2 teaspoons of the salt. Pulse several times, scraping down the sides of the bowl as necessary, until the garlic is finely minced. Add 1 tablespoon (15ml) of lemon juice and pulse again until a paste forms. With the motor running, slowly add 120ml of the oil in a steady stream. Add an additional tablespoon (15ml) of lemon juice and pulse. Then, with the motor running, slowly add a second 120 ml of oil followed by the third tablespoon (15ml) of lemon juice. 3. Repeat this process until you have used all the oil. Transfer the toum, which should be fluffy and similar in texture to a mousse, to a serving bowl or container, if not using right away, and refrigerate until needed. 4. Drain the potatoes and pat dry. Toss with the remaining 1 tablespoon (15 ml) of oil and remaining teaspoon of salt. Preheat the air fryer to 190°C. Working in batches of 2 or 3, arrange the fries in a single layer in the air fryer basket, taking care not to crowd them, and cook for 22 to 25 minutes, shaking and turning every 5 minutes or so, until the potatoes are browned on all sides and crispy. Repeat with the remaining fries. 5. Toss the potatoes with additional salt, if desired. Serve the steak fries immediately with toum for dipping.
**Per Serving:** Calories 254; Fat 7.9g; Sodium 2544mg; Carbs 2g; Fibre 10g; Sugar 6g; Protein 11g

# Herbed Mushroom Frittata

**Prep time: 10 minutes | Cook time:40 minutes | Serves:4**

35g Grated Manchego cheese
5 eggs
1 small onion, diced finely
2 stalks of green garlic, peeled and minced
150g chopped white mushrooms
1 tablespoon dried basil

120ml of olive oil
¼ teaspoon Oregano, dry
1 tablespoon of fresh Italian flat-leaf parsley
½ teaspoon of dried parsley flakes
1 teaspoon of powdered porcini
To enjoy: table salt and freshly ground black pepper

1. Set your Air Fryer to 175°C to begin. To the baking dish for the Air Fryer, add the oil, mushrooms, onion, and green garlic. This mixture should be baked for 6 minutes, or until soft. 2. In the meantime, crack the eggs into a mixing basin and whisk them vigorously. Remix after adding the seasonings. Remove the baking pan from the oven. 3. In the baking dish with the sautéed mixture, pour the whisked egg mixture. Add some shredded Manchego cheese on top. 4. Your frittata should be baked for about 32 minutes at 160°C or until it has set. Serve hot.
**Per Serving:** Calories 260, Fat 19.59g; Sodium 377mg; Carbs 6.1g; Fibre 0.9g; Sugar 2.33g; Protein 15.02g

# Sweet Potatoes Glazed in Tamarind

**Prep time: 10 minutes | Cook time: 24 minutes | Serves:4**

⅓ teaspoon. white pepper
1 teaspoon melted butter
½ teaspoon of turmeric powder
5 chopped garnet sweet potatoes, each peeled

A few liquid droplets Stevia
1½ tablespoons of fresh lime juice
2 teaspoons of tamarind paste
1½ teaspoons of allspice, ground

1. Toss all the ingredients in a mixing dish until the sweet potatoes are thoroughly covered. 2. Fry them for 12 minutes in the air at 170°C. 3. Restart the Air Fryer after pausing it. Cook for a further 10 minutes at a higher temperature of 200°C. Eat warm.
**Per Serving:** Calories 190, Fat 10.13g; Sodium 637mg; Carbs 19.39g; Fibre 2.1g; Sugar 2.2g; Protein 6.61g

# Fried Pickles

**Prep time: 10 minutes | Cook time: 20 minutes | Serves:6**

80ml of milk
1 teaspoon of powdered garlic
2 eggs of medium size
1 teaspoon of sea salt, fine

⅓ teaspoon of chili powder
40g plain flour
⅛ teaspoon powdered shallot
2 jars Sweet and sour pickle spears

1. With a kitchen towel, dry the pickle spears. Afterward, get two mixing bowls. 2. In a bowl, combine the egg and milk. All dry ingredients should be combined in another bowl. 3. The pickle spears should first be dipped into the dry mixture, then into the egg or milk mixture, and then back into the dry mixture for a second coating. 4. Air-fried battered pickles for 15 minutes at 195°C. Enjoy!
**Per Serving:** Calories 58, Fat 1.96g; Sodium 513mg; Carbs 6.76g; Fibre 0.4g; Sugar 0.91g; Protein 3.14g

# Croquettes of Fried Squash

**Prep time: 10 minutes | Cook time: 22 minutes | Serves:4**

40g plain flour
⅓ teaspoon freshly ground black pepper, or as desired
⅓ teaspoon of dried sage
4 minced garlic cloves
1½ tablespoons of olive oil

⅓ of a grated and peeled butternut squash
2 well-whisked eggs
1 teaspoon of sea salt, fine
A dash of allspice, ground

1. In a mixing basin, thoroughly combine all the ingredients. 2. Set your Air Fryer's temperature to 175°C, then cook your fritters for 17 minutes or until they are golden brown. 3. Then, serve right immediately.
**Per Serving:** Calories 190, Fat 10.13g; Sodium 637mg; Carbs 19.39g; Fibre 2.1g; Sugar 2.2g; Protein 6.61g

# Roasted Cauliflower with Pepper Jack Cheese

**Prep time: 10 minutes | Cook time: 25 minutes | Serves: 2**

⅓ teaspoon powdered shallot
1 teaspoon of black pepper, ground
1½ large cauliflower heads, divided into florets
¼ teaspoon of cumin powder

½ teaspoon garlic salt
25g grated Pepper Jack cheese
1½ tablespoons Vegetable oil
⅓ teaspoon Paprika

1. In a big pot of salted water, boil the cauliflower for around five minutes. After that, drain the cauliflower florets. 2. In a bowl, combine the remaining ingredients, including the cauliflower florets. Transfer them to a baking dish. 3. They should be roasted for 16 minutes at 200°C, turning them once. Enjoy!
**Per Serving:** Calories 199, Fat 15.33g; Sodium 146mg; Carbs 11.6g; Fibre 4.5g; Sugar 3.95g; Protein 7.53g

# Spicy Cauliflower Balls

**Prep time: 10 minutes | Cook time: 48 minutes | Serves: 6**

2 tablespoons Chili powder
1½ teaspoons salt
1 teaspoon crumbled dried marjoram
270g of floretized cauliflower

50g of crumbed tortilla chips
½ teaspoon of red pepper flakes, crushed
Whisked 3 eggs
370g feta cheese, crumbled

1. Cauliflower florets should be processed in a food processor until they are crushed (it is the size of rice). After that, add the other ingredients with the cauliflower "rice." 2. The cauliflower mixture should now be formed into small balls and chilled for 30 minutes. 3. Set your Air Fryer's temperature to 175°C and a timer for 14 minutes. Cook the balls until they are golden, then serve right immediately.
**Per Serving:** Calories 220, Fat 15.48g; Sodium 1111mg; Carbs 8.67g; Fibre 1.5g; Sugar 1.33g; Protein 11.89g

# Omelet with Cheese and Mixed Greens

**Prep time: 10 minutes | Cook time: 17 minutes | Serves: 2**

80g of cheese, ricotta
5 beaten eggs
½ cut and seeded red pepper
100g of roughly chopped mixed greens

½ of a sliced, seeded green pepper
½ teaspoon of dried basil
½ of chipotle pepper, minced
½ teaspoon of dried oregano

1. Apply a thin layer of pan spray into a baking dish. 2. After that, combine all the ingredients in the baking dish and stir well. 3. Bake for 15 minutes at 160°C.

**Per Serving:** Calories 414, Fat 29.54g; Sodium 336mg; Carbs 7.99g; Fibre 1.4g; Sugar 3.59g; Protein 28.17g

# Spicy Corn on Cob

**Prep Time: 10 minutes | Cook Time: 16 minutes | Serves: 4**

Olive oil
2 tablespoons grated Parmesan cheese
1 teaspoon chili powder
1 teaspoon garlic powder
1 teaspoon ground cumin

1 teaspoon paprika
1 teaspoon salt
¼ teaspoon cayenne pepper, optional
4 ears fresh corn, shucked

1. Lightly spray the air fryer basket with olive oil. 2. Mix the Parmesan cheese, chili powder, garlic powder, cumin, paprika, salt, and cayenne pepper in a bowl. 3. Lightly spray the ears of corn with olive oil, and sprinkle them with the seasoning mixture. 4. Place the ears of corn in the air fryer basket in a single layer. 5. Air fry the ears of corn at 205°C for 7 minutes. 6. Turn the corn over and air fry for 7 to 9 minutes more until lightly browned. 7. Serve warm.

**Per Serving:** Calories 142; Fat 2.7g; Sodium 669mg; Carbs 29.06g; Fibre 4.5g; Sugar 4.76g; Protein 5.72g

# Bacon with Brussels Sprouts

**Prep Time: 10 minutes | Cook Time: 10 minutes | Serves: 4**

Olive oil
400g fresh Brussels sprouts, trimmed and halved
1 tablespoon crumbled cooked bacon
2 teaspoons balsamic vinegar

1 teaspoon olive oil
1 teaspoon salt
1 teaspoon pepper

1. Lightly spray the air fryer basket with olive oil. 2. Toss the Brussels sprouts with the crumbled bacon, balsamic vinegar, olive oil, salt, and pepper in a bowl. 3. Place the Brussels sprouts in the air fryer basket. 4. Air fry them at 175°C for 10 minutes until they are fork-tender and lightly browned, shaking the basket and lightly spraying with the olive oil halfway through. 5. Serve.

**Per Serving:** Calories 73; Fat 2.15g; Sodium 644mg; Carbs 11.81g; Fibre 4.5g; Sugar 3.46g; Protein 4.31g

# Roasted Broccoli

**Prep Time: 5 minutes | Cook Time: 12 minutes | Serves: 4**

1½ teaspoons olive oil, plus more for spraying
455g broccoli

1 tablespoon everything bagel seasoning

1. Lightly spray the air fryer basket with olive oil. 2. In a large bowl, toss the broccoli with the ½ tablespoon olive oil and everything bagel seasoning. 3. Place the broccoli in the air fryer basket in a single layer. 4. Air fry the broccoli at 190°C for 8 to 12 minutes until they are tender and lightly browned, shaking the basket after 5 minutes of cooking. You can cook them in batches. 5. Serve warm.

**Per Serving:** Calories 101; Fat 2.63g; Sodium 145mg; Carbs 15.21g; Fibre 4.1g; Sugar 1.93g; Protein 6.09g

# Roasted Tomatoes

**Prep Time: 10 minutes | Cook Time: 6 minutes | Serves: 4**

Olive oil
4 Roma tomatoes, cut into 1 cm slices
Salt
60g shredded mozzarella cheese

25g shredded Parmesan cheese
Freshly ground black pepper
Parsley flakes

1. Lightly spray the air fryer basket with olive oil. 2. Lightly season the tomato slices with salt. 3. Place the tomato slices in the air fryer basket in a single layer. 4. Sprinkle each tomato slice with 1 teaspoon of mozzarella cheese, and top each with ½ teaspoon of shredded Parmesan cheese, then season them with black pepper and sprinkle parsley flakes. 5. Air fry them at 190°C for 5 to 6 minutes until the cheese is melted, bubbly, and lightly browned. 6. Serve warm.
**Per Serving:** Calories 74; Fat 3.07g; Sodium 261mg; Carbs 5.29g; Fibre 1.5g; Sugar 2.61g; Protein 7.12g

# Breaded Pepper Strips

**Prep Time: 15 minutes | Cook Time: 7 minutes | Serves: 4**

Olive oil
65g whole-wheat panko bread crumbs
½ teaspoon paprika
½ teaspoon garlic powder

½ teaspoon salt
1 egg, beaten
2 red, orange, or yellow peppers, cut into 1 cm-thick slices

1. Lightly spray the air fryer basket with olive oil. 2. In a medium shallow bowl, mix together the panko bread crumbs, paprika, garlic powder, and salt. 3. In another small shallow bowl, whisk the egg with 1½ teaspoons of water to make an egg wash. 4. Dip the pepper slices in the egg wash to coat, then dredge them in the panko bread crumbs until evenly coated. 5. Place the pepper slices in the fryer basket in a single layer. Lightly spray the pepper strips with oil. 6. Air fry them at 205°C for 4 to 7 minutes until lightly browned. 7. Carefully remove from fryer basket to ensure that the coating does not come off. Serve immediately.
**Per Serving:** Calories 143; Fat 3.03g; Sodium 319mg; Carbs 22.23g; Fibre 1.5g; Sugar 0.27g; Protein 6.03g

# Flavourful Broccoli

**Prep Time: 10 minutes | Cook Time: 20 minutes | Serves: 4**

½ teaspoon olive oil, plus more for spraying
455g fresh broccoli, cut into florets
½ tablespoon minced garlic
Salt
1½ tablespoons soy sauce

1 teaspoon white vinegar
2 teaspoons hot sauce or sriracha
1½ teaspoons honey
Freshly ground black pepper

1. Lightly spray the air fryer basket with olive oil. 2. In a large bowl, Toss the broccoli florets with ½ teaspoon of olive oil and the minced garlic, and then season them with salt. 3. Place the broccoli in the fryer basket in a single layer. 4. Air fry them at 205°C for 15 to 20 minutes until lightly browned and crispy, shaking the basket every 5 minutes. Do the same with the remaining broccoli. 5. In a small bowl, whisk together the soy sauce, white vinegar, hot sauce, honey, and black pepper. If the honey doesn't incorporate well, microwave the mixture for 10 to 20 seconds until the honey melts. 6. In a large bowl, toss the cooked broccoli with the sauce mixture, and season with additional salt and pepper, if desired. 7. Serve immediately.
**Per Serving:** Calories 58; Fat 2.23g; Sodium 229mg; Carbs 7.33g; Fibre 3.2g; Sugar 3.8g; Protein 4.11g

# Delicious Broccoli Cheese Tots

**Prep Time: 20 minutes | Cook Time: 15 minutes | Serves: 4**

Olive oil
300g frozen broccoli, thawed and drained
1 large egg
1½ teaspoons minced garlic
25g grated Parmesan cheese

25g shredded reduced-fat sharp Cheddar cheese
50g seasoned whole-wheat bread crumbs
Salt
Freshly ground black pepper

1. Lightly spray the air fryer basket with olive oil. 2. Gently squeeze the thawed broccoli to remove any excess liquid. 3. Add the broccoli, egg, garlic, Parmesan cheese, Cheddar cheese, bread crumbs, salt, and pepper to the food processor, and pulse until it resembles a coarse meal. 4. Scoop up the broccoli mixture and shape into 24 ovals "tater tot" shapes. 5. Place the tots in the air fryer basket in a single layer, being careful to space them a little bit apart. Lightly spray the tots with oil. 6. Air fry them at 190°C for 6 to 7 minutes, turning the tots over and cook for an additional 6 to 8 minutes or until lightly browned and crispy. 7. Serve and enjoy.
**Per Serving:** Calories 107; Fat 5.71g; Sodium 235mg; Carbs 8.25g; Fibre 2.7g; Sugar 1.56g; Protein 7.23g

# Roasted Peppers with Parsley

**Prep time: 10 minutes | Cook time: 11 minutes | Serves: 4**

1 red pepper, sliced
1 yellow pepper, sliced
1 orange pepper, sliced
1 tablespoon olive oil
1 teaspoon freshly squeezed lemon juice

1 teaspoon dried Italian seasoning
½ teaspoon sea salt
⅛ teaspoon freshly ground black pepper
10g chopped fresh flat-leaf parsley

1. Combine the peppers in the air fryer basket. Drizzle with the olive oil and lemon juice, and sprinkle with the Italian seasoning, salt, and pepper. Toss to coat. Place the basket in the air fryer. 2. Set or preheat the air fryer to 175°C. Roast for 8 to 11 minutes, shaking once during cooking time, until the peppers are tender and starting to brown around the edges. 3. Sprinkle with the parsley and serve.
**Per Serving:** Calories 57; Fat 3.6g; Sodium 353mg; Carbs 6g; Fibre 1.2g; Sugar 1.3g; Protein 1.3g

# Chapter 3 Fish and Seafood Recipes

# Tasty Cajun Prawn and Veggies

**Prep Time: 10 minutes | Cook Time: 15 minutes | Serves: 6**

455 g jumbo prawn, peeled and deveined
2 medium courgette, cut into 1 cm slices, then cut in half
2 peppers (red, yellow, or orange), cut into 2.5 cm chunks
2 tablespoons Cajun seasoning

2 tablespoons extra-virgin olive oil, plus more for the air fryer basket
2 fully cooked smoked turkey sausages, cut into 1 cm slices

1. Turn on and preheat the air fryer to 205°C. 2. Toss in a large bowl the prawn, courgette, and peppers with the Cajun seasoning and olive oil. Stir in the smoked sausage slices. 3. Sprinkle the air fryer basket with oil lightly. Put the seasoned prawn, vegetables, and sausages in a single layer in the air fryer basket. 4. Air fry for 15 minutes, shaking the air fryer basket every 5 minutes until the vegetables are tender and seared..
**Per Serving:** Calories 137; Fat 5.93g; Sodium 904mg; Carbs 3.24g; Fibre 0.7g; Sugar 1.21g; Protein 16.45g

# Indulgent Lobster Tails with Butter and Lemon

**Prep Time: 10 minutes | Cook Time: 10 minutes | Serves: 2**

2 lobster tails
Extra-virgin olive oil, for greasing the air fryer basket
2 tablespoons butter, melted, plus more for serving

(optional)
Salt
1 lemon, cut into wedges

1. Turn on and preheat the air fryer to 205°C. 2. Use kitchen scissors to cut the lobster tails from open end to the tail fins. Do not cut through the tail fins. Spread open the shell with your fingers and push the meat upward so it separates from the bottom shell. Leave the end attached at the tail fin. Hold the lobster meat up and push the shell together under the meat. Place the meat on the top of the shell. 3. Sprinkle the air fryer basket with oil lightly. Put the lobster tails in a single layer in the air fryer basket. Pour the melted butter over the lobster meat and season with salt. 4. Air fry them for 6 to 8 minutes until the lobster reaches an internal temperature of 60°C. 5. Serve the dish with lemon wedges and extra melted butter (optional).
**Per Serving:** Calories 242; Fat 14.95g; Sodium 1889mg; Carbs 1.66g; Fibre 0.1g; Sugar 0.61g; Protein 24.98g

# Delicious Fish and Chips

**Prep Time: 25 minutes | Cook Time: 35 minutes | Serves: 4**

**For Chips**
2 large russet potatoes, scrubbed
1 tablespoon extra-virgin olive oil, plus more for greasing the air fryer basket
**For Fish**
4 (100 g) white fish fillets, such as pollock, cod, or haddock
1½ teaspoons salt, divided, plus more for seasoning
1½ teaspoons black pepper, divided, plus more for seasoning
60 g plain flour

1 teaspoon seasoned salt
½ teaspoon freshly ground black pepper

2 large eggs
1 teaspoon water
160 g panko bread crumbs
¼ teaspoon cayenne pepper
Extra-virgin olive oil, for spraying

1. Turn on and preheat the air fryer to 205°C. 2. Cut the potatoes lengthwise into 1 cm thick slices and then again into 1-cm-thick fries. 3. Mix in a large bowl the olive oil with the seasoned salt and pepper, then add the fries and toss to coat. 4. Sprinkle the air fryer basket with oil lightly. Put the fries in a single layer in the air fryer basket. 5. Air fry them for 5 minutes; shake the air fryer basket and air fry for another 5 to 10 minutes. Set aside and keep warm. 6. Season the fish fillets with salt and black pepper. 7. Mix in a small shallow bowl together the flour, ½ teaspoon salt, and ½ teaspoon black pepper. 8. In a second shallow bowl, whisk together the eggs and a pinch each of salt and black pepper. 9. Combine in another bowl the bread crumbs, cayenne pepper, remaining 1 teaspoon salt, and remaining 1 teaspoon black pepper. 10. Turn on and preheat the air fryer to 205°C. 11. Coat each fillet in the seasoned flour, then in the egg, then in the breading. 12. Sprinkle the air fryer basket with oil lightly. Put the coated fillets in a single layer in the air fryer basket. Lightly spray with oil. 13. Air fry them for 8 to 10 minutes; flip the fillets and lightly spray with oil, and air fry them for an another 5 to 10 minutes.
**Per Serving:** Calories 455; Fat 11. 27g; Sodium 1595mg; Carbs 53.02g; Fibre 3.6g; Sugar 2g; Protein 34.88g

# Wonderful Fried Catfish

**Prep Time: 10 minutes | Cook Time: 20 minutes | Serves: 4**

240 ml buttermilk
4 catfish fillets
170 g polenta

1 tablespoon Creole seasoning
Extra-virgin olive oil, for spraying

1. Pour the buttermilk into a shallow baking dish. Put the catfish in the dish, cover, and refrigerate for at least 1 hour. 2. Turn on and preheat the air fryer to 205°C. 3. Combine the polenta and Creole seasoning in a small bowl. 4. Take the catfish out of the dish and shake off any excess buttermilk. Put each fillet in the polenta mixture. Press on the polenta to ensure it adheres. 5. Sprinkle the air fryer basket with oil lightly. Put the coated catfish strips in a single layer in the air fryer basket. Lightly spray them with oil. 6. Air fry the catfish strips for 7 to 10 minutes; flip the catfish and lightly spray with oil, and air fry for an another 8 to 10 minutes. 7. When done, they should be golden brown and crispy.
**Per Serving:** Calories 338; Fat 6.83g; Sodium 342mg; Carbs 35.37g; Fibre 1.8g; Sugar 3.8g; Protein 30.96g

# Flaky Chile-Lime Tilapia

**Prep Time: 10 minutes | Cook Time: 15 minutes | Serves: 4**

4 teaspoons chili powder
2 teaspoons ground cumin
2 teaspoons garlic powder
1 teaspoon salt

½ teaspoon freshly ground black pepper
4 (125 g – 150 g) tilapia fillets
Extra-virgin olive oil, for the parchment paper
2 limes, cut into wedges

1. Turn on and preheat the air fryer to 195°C. 2. Combine in a small bowl the chili powder, cumin, garlic powder, salt, and pepper. 3. Pat the tilapia fillets dry with a paper towel. 4. Press the spice mixture all over the fish. 5. Line the air fryer basket with a sheet of perforated parchment paper, and lightly spray the parchment with oil. 6. Put the seasoned fillets in a single layer in the air fryer basket, leaving 1 cm of space between each to ensure even cooking. 7. Air fry the fillets for 10 to 15 minutes until flake easily. 8. Drizzle lime juice over the top, and enjoy.
**Per Serving:** Calories 144; Fat 3.75g; Sodium 722mg; Carbs 4.98g; Fibre 1.4g; Sugar 0.63g; Protein24.22g

# Delicious Bacon-Wrapped Scallops

**Prep Time: 5 minutes | Cook Time: 10 minutes | Serves: 4**

455 g jumbo sea scallops
455 g sliced bacon

Extra-virgin olive oil, for the air fryer basket
Freshly ground black pepper

1. Turn on and preheat the air fryer to 205°C. 2. Pat the scallops dry with paper towels and remove any side muscles. 3. Cut the bacon slices in half so you have half a slice for each scallop. 4. Wrap each scallop in bacon and secure the bacon with a toothpick. 5. Sprinkle the air fryer basket with oil lightly. Put the bacon-wrapped scallops in a single layer in the air fryer basket. 6. Air fry for 8 minutes. Flip the scallops and season with pepper. Air fry for another 4 minutes until the scallops are tender and opaque.
**Per Serving:** Calories 599; Fat 46.63g; Sodium 1289mg; Carbs 7.44g; Fibre 0.1g; Sugar 0.94g; Protein 37.56g

# Air Fryer Salmon with Creamy Sauce

**Prep time: 10 minutes | Cook time: 10 minutes | Serves 2**

340 g salmon, cut into 6 pieces
Salt
60 g plain yogurt

1 tablespoon dill, chopped
3 tablespoons light sour cream
1 tablespoon olive oil

1. Spice the salmon with salt and place it in air fryer. 2. Drizzle the salmon with olive oil. Air-fry salmon at 140°C and cook for 10-minutes. 3. Mix the dill, yogurt, sour cream and some salt. 4. Place salmon on serving dish and drizzle with creamy sauce.
**Per Serving:** Calories 789; Fat 7.9g; Sodium 412mg; Carbs 2g; Fibre 69g; Sugar 47g; Protein 12g

# Delicious Fried Prawn

**Prep Time: 15 minutes | Cook Time: 15 minutes | Serves: 4**

2 teaspoons Old Bay seasoning, divided
½ teaspoon garlic powder
½ teaspoon onion powder
½ teaspoon freshly ground black pepper
455 g large prawn, deveined, tails on

2 large eggs
1 teaspoon water
55 g panko bread crumbs
Extra-virgin olive oil, for spraying

1. Turn on and preheat the air fryer to 195°C. 2. Mix in a medium bowl together 1 teaspoon Old Bay, the garlic powder, onion powder, and pepper. Add the prawns and toss to coat lightly. 3. Whisk in a small bowl the eggs with the water. 4. Mix the remaining 1 teaspoon Old Bay and the bread crumbs in a small shallow bowl. 5. Coat each prawn in the egg mixture, then the breading. 6. Sprinkle the air fryer basket with oil lightly. Put the prawns in a single layer in the air fryer basket. Do not overcrowd. Lightly spray with oil. 7. Air fry for 10 to 15 minutes, shaking the air fryer basket every 5 minutes.
**Per Serving:** Calories 134; Fat 4.71g; Sodium 668mg; Carbs 4.44g; Fibre 0.4g; Sugar 0.33g; Protein 17.32g

# Quick Lemon-Garlic Jumbo Scallops

**Prep Time: 10 minutes | Cook Time: 10 minutes | Serves: 4**

4 tablespoons unsalted butter, melted
2 tablespoons freshly squeezed lemon juice
1 tablespoon minced garlic
½ teaspoon salt

⅛ teaspoon freshly ground black pepper
455 g jumbo sea scallops
Extra-virgin olive oil, for the air fryer basket

1. Turn on and preheat the air fryer to 205°C. 2. Combine the melted butter, lemon juice, garlic, salt, and pepper in a medium bowl. 3. Add the sea scallops and toss to coat. 4. Sprinkle the air fryer basket with oil lightly. Put the scallops in a single layer in the air fryer basket. 5. Air fry for 8 minutes, flipping after 4 minutes.
**Per Serving:** Calories 211; Fat 9.82g; Sodium 1053mg; Carbs 7.41g; Fibre 0.1g; Sugar 0.21g; Protein 23.92g

# Tropical Coconut Prawns

**Prep time: 10 minutes | Cook time: 10 minutes | Serves 4**

100 g breadcrumbs
100 g dried coconut, unsweetened
100 g almond flour

Sea salt
900 g. prawns
240 g egg whites

1. In a mixing bowl, combine coconut and breadcrumbs. Spice lightly with sea salt. 2. In another bowl, add flour, and in a third bowl, add egg whites. 3. Preheat your air fryer to 170°C. Dip each prawns into flour, egg whites, then the breadcrumbs. 4. Cook the prawns for 10-minutes and serve with preferred dipping sauce.
**Per Serving:** Calories 321; Fat 7.9g; Sodium 789mg; Carbs 741g; Fibre 87g; Sugar 29g; Protein 93g

# Spicy Cajun Prawns

**Prep time: 5 minutes | Cook time: 5 minutes | Serves 4**

570 g prawns, peeled and deveined
¼ teaspoon salt
½ teaspoon paprika

1 tablespoon olive oil
¼ cayenne pepper
½ teaspoon Old Bay seasoning

1. Preheat air fryer to 205°C. Mix all the ingredients in a bowl. Place the spiced prawns into air fryer basket and cook for 5-minutes.
**Per Serving:** Calories222; Fat 7g; Sodium 634mg; Carbs 9g; Fibre 85g; Sugar 78g; Protein 32g

# Great Garlic-Ginger Salmon

**Prep Time: 10 minutes | Cook Time: 10 minutes | Serves: 4**

60 ml soy sauce
2 tablespoons extra-virgin olive oil, plus more for the parchment paper
2 tablespoons grated fresh ginger

1 tablespoon minced garlic
1 tablespoon balsamic vinegar
4 (100 g) boneless, skinless salmon fillets

1. In a medium bowl, whisk the soy sauce, olive oil, ginger, garlic, and balsamic vinegar. 2. Put the salmon fillets in the marinade, then cover the bowl, and refrigerate them for at least 30 minutes but no longer than 3 hours. 3. Turn on and preheat the air fryer to 180°C. 4. Put a sheet of air fryer perforated parchment paper in the air fryer basket and lightly spray with oil. Put the marinated salmon fillets in a single layer in the air fryer basket. 5. Air fry the salmon fillets for 6 minutes; flip the fillets and air fry for an another 4 to 6 minutes until they have an internal temperature of 60°C.
**Per Serving:** Calories 129; Fat 8.46g; Sodium 1083mg; Carbs 8.84g; Fibre 0.7g; Sugar 2.5g; Protein 4.73g

# Delicious Crab Croquettes

**Prep time: 10 minutes | Cook time: 18 minutes | Serves 6**

455 g crab meat
100 g breadcrumbs
2 egg whites
Salt and black pepper
½ teaspoon parsley, chopped
¼ teaspoon chives
¼ teaspoon tarragon

2 tablespoons celeries, chopped
4 tablespoons mayonnaise
4 tablespoons light sour cream
1 teaspoon olive oil
½ teaspoon lime juice
75 g red pepper, chopped
35 g onion, chopped

1. Preheat your air fryer to 180°C. Add breadcrumbs with salt and pepper. 2. In another bowl, add the egg whites. 3. Add all the remaining ingredients into a third bowl and mix well. 4. Make croquettes from crab mixture and dip into egg whites, and then into breadcrumbs. Place into air fryer and cook for 18-minutes.
**Per Serving:** Calories 458; Fat 7.9g; Sodium 258mg; Carbs 8g; Fibre 64g; Sugar 14g; Protein 78g

# Easy Fried Cod Fillets

**Prep time: 10 minutes | Cook time: 12 minutes | Serves 5**

2 large eggs, beaten
3 tablespoons milk
200 g breadcrumbs

455 g cod fillets
100 g almond meal
Salt and pepper

1. In a bowl, mix egg and milk. In a dish, combine breadcrumbs, pepper, and salt. 2. In another dish, add the almond meal. Roll the cod sticks into almond meal, dip in egg, and coat in breadcrumbs. 3. Place the coated cod sticks in air fryer basket. Air fry at 175°Cfor 12-minutes and shake basket halfway through cook time. Serve hot.
**Per Serving:** Calories 254; Fat 7.9g; Sodium 2544mg; Carbs 2g; Fibre 10g; Sugar 6g; Protein 11g

# Barbecued Prawns

**Prep time: 10 minutes | Cook time: 15 minutes | Serves 4**

680 g of prawns
360 g barbeque sauce

1 fresh lime, cut into litreers

1. Preheat your air fryer to 180°C. 2. Place the prawns in a bowl with barbeque sauce. Stir gently. Allow prawns to marinade for at least 5-minutes. 3. Place the prawns in air fryer and cook for 15-minutes. Remove from air fryer and squeeze lime over prawns s.
**Per Serving:** Calories 321; Fat 7.9g; Sodium 789mg; Carbs 741g; Fibre 87g; Sugar 29g; Protein 93g

# Coconut Crab Buns

**Prep time: 15 minutes | Cook time: 20 minutes | Serves: 2**

2 tablespoons coconut flour
¼ teaspoon baking powder
125g crab meat, chopped
2 eggs, beaten

1 tablespoon coconut oil, softened
½ teaspoon coconut aminos
½ teaspoon ground black pepper

1. Combine the crab meat, eggs, coconut flour, baking powder, coconut aminos, coarsely powdered black pepper, and coconut oil in a mixing bowl. 2. Knead the silky dough and chop it up. 3. Form the crab mixture into buns and place them in the air fryer basket. 4. Bake the crab buns at 185°C for 20 minutes.
**Per Serving:** Calories 418, Fat 18.6g; Sodium 128 mg; Carbs 30.16g; Fibre 12.8g; Sugar 1.65g; Protein 36.33g

# Tilapia with Chili and Oregano

**Prep time: 5 minutes | Cook time: 20 minutes | Serves: 4**

1 teaspoon chili flakes
4 tilapia fillets, boneless
1 teaspoon mustard

1 teaspoon dried oregano
1 tablespoon avocado oil

1. Before placing the tilapia fillets in the air fryer, season them with mustard, avocado oil, dried oregano, and chili flakes. 2. At 180°C, cook it for 10 minutes on each side.
**Per Serving:** Calories 146, Fat 5.62g; Sodium 94mg; Carbs 0.58g; Fibre 0.4g; Sugar 0.07g; Protein 23.45g

# Haddock in Cream

**Prep time: 10 minutes | Cook time: 8 minutes | Serves: 4**

455g haddock fillet
1 teaspoon cayenne pepper
1 teaspoon salt

1 teaspoon coconut oil
120g heavy cream

1. Use coconut oil to coat the baking dish. 2. Next, place the haddock fillet inside and top with heavy cream, salt, and cayenne pepper. 3. Place the baking pan in the basket of the air fryer, and cook for 8 minutes at 190°C.
**Per Serving:** Calories 147, Fat 7.26g; Sodium 829mg; Carbs 0.67g; Fibre 0.1g; Sugar 0.47g; Protein 18.87g

# Simple Fish Sticks

**Prep time: 15 minutes | Cook time: 15 minutes | Serves: 4**

Olive oil
4 fish fillets (cod, tilapia or pollock)
65g whole-wheat flour
1 teaspoon seasoned salt

2 eggs
155g whole-wheat panko bread crumbs
½ tablespoon dried parsley flakes

1. Spray an air fryer basket lightly with olive oil. 2. Cut the fish fillets lengthwise into "sticks." 3. In a shallow bowl, mix together the whole-wheat flour and seasoned salt. 4. In a small bowl whisk the eggs with 1 teaspoon of water. 5. Mix the panko bread crumbs and parsley flakes in another shallow bowl. 6. Coat each fish stick in the seasoned flour, then in the egg mixture, and dredge them in the panko bread crumbs. 7. Lay the fish sticks evenly in the air fryer basket in a single layer and lightly spray the fish sticks with olive oil. Work in batches as needed. 8. Air fry the fish sticks at 205°C for 5 to 8 minutes. Flip the fish sticks over and lightly spray with the olive oil. Cook until golden brown and crispy, for 5 to 7 more minutes.
**Per Serving:** Calories 490; Fat 13.3g; Sodium 1107mg; Carbs 49g; Fibre 2.9g; Sugar 0.7g; Protein 41g

# Cod with Jalapeno

**Prep time: 5 minutes | Cook time: 14 minutes | Serves: 4**

4 cod fillets, boneless
1 jalapeno, minced

1 tablespoon avocado oil
½ teaspoon minced garlic

1. Combine the minced jalapeno, avocado oil, and minced garlic in a small bowl. 2. Arrange the cod fillets in a single layer in the air fryer basket, then top with the minced jalapeno mixture. 3. Cook the fish for 7 minutes on each side at 185°C.
**Per Serving:** Calories 113, Fat 3.99g; Sodium 352mg; Carbs 0.34g; Fibre 0.1g; Sugar 0.15g; Protein 17.77g

# Spinach Stuffed Mackerel

**Prep time: 15 minutes | Cook time: 20 minutes | Serves: 5**

455g mackerel, trimmed
1 pepper, chopped
15g spinach, chopped

1 tablespoon avocado oil
1 teaspoon ground black pepper
1 teaspoon tomato paste

1. Combine the pepper, spinach, tomato paste, and coarsely ground black pepper in a mixing dish. 2. Fill the mackerel with spinach mixture. 3. Next, fried the fish in the air fryer after brushing it with avocado oil. 4. Cook the fish for 20 minutes at 185°C.
**Per Serving:** Calories 128, Fat 4.67g; Sodium 148 mg; Carbs 1.93g; Fibre 0.4g; Sugar 1.01g; Protein 18.87g

# Spicy Cod Pan

**Prep time: 5 minutes | Cook time: 12 minutes | Serves: 4**

455g cod fillet, chopped
1 teaspoon coconut oil
1 teaspoon chili flakes

½ teaspoon cayenne pepper
1 teaspoon dried coriander
¼ teaspoon ground nutmeg

1. Rub the coconut oil, chili flakes, cayenne, dried coriander, and crushed nutmeg into the cod fillet. 2. Place the fillets in the air fryer and heat to 185°C for 6 minutes on each side.
**Per Serving:** Calories 250, Fat 13.86g; Sodium 82mg; Carbs 0.54g; Fibre 0.3g; Sugar 0.08g; Protein 29.17g

# Fried Marinated Salmon Fillets

**Prep time: 1 hour 10 minutes | Cook time: 20 minutes | Serves: 4**

1 tablespoon olive oil, plus more for spraying
60ml soy sauce
60ml rice wine vinegar
1 tablespoon brown sugar
1 teaspoon mustard powder

1 teaspoon ground ginger
½ teaspoon freshly ground black pepper
½ teaspoon minced garlic
4 (150g) salmon fillets, skin-on

1. Spray an air fryer basket lightly with olive oil. 2. Combine the brown sugar, the soy sauce, rice wine vinegar, brown sugar, 1 tablespoon of olive oil, mustard powder, ginger, black pepper, and garlic in a small bowl to make a marinade. 3. Place the fillets in a shallow baking dish and pour the marinade over them. Cover the baking dish and then refrigerate it for at least 1 hour, turning the fillets occasionally to keep them well coated in the marinade. 4. Shake off as much marinade as possible from the fillets and place them in the air fryer basket in a single layer, skin side down. Cook the fillets in batches as needed. 5. Air fry the fillets at 185°C for 10 to 15 minutes for medium-rare to medium done salmon or 15 to 20 minutes for well done. The minimum internal temperature should be 60°C at the thickest part of the fillet.
**Per Serving:** Calories 295; Fat 12.7g; Sodium 341mg; Carbs 6.8g; Fibre 0.5g; Sugar 5.1g; Protein 35.5g

# Coconut Sardines

**Prep time: 15 minutes | Cook time: 10 minutes | Serves: 5**

300g sardines, trimmed, cleaned
125g coconut flour

1 tablespoon coconut oil
1 teaspoon salt

1. Before coating the sardines in coconut flour, salt them. 2. After that, coat the air fryer basket with coconut oil and add the sardines. 3. Prepare them for 10 minutes at 195°C.

**Per Serving:** Calories 174, Fat 10.61g; Sodium 724mg; Carbs 1.78g; Fibre 0.5g; Sugar 1.25g; Protein 17.1g

# Simple Basil Prawns

**Prep time: 5 minutes | Cook time: 12 minutes | Serves: 4**

1 teaspoon dried basil
455g prawns, peeled

1 tablespoon avocado oil
½ teaspoon salt

1. Combine salt, dried basil, and avocado oil with the prawns. 2. Layer them in the air fryer and cook for 12 minutes at 185°C.

**Per Serving:** Calories 145, Fat 5.05g; Sodium 1277mg; Carbs 0.08g; Fibre 0.1g; Sugar 0g; Protein 23.2g

# Bacon Wrapped Halibut

**Prep time: 15 minutes | Cook time: 10 minutes | Serves: 2**

1 teaspoon ground black pepper
2 150g halibut steaks

1 teaspoon avocado oil
100g bacon, sliced

1. Season the halibut steaks with freshly ground black pepper and avocado oil. 2. After that, wrap the fish in bacon pieces and air fry it. 3. Cook the fish for five minutes on each side at 200°C.

**Per Serving:** Calories 556, Fat 39.61g; Sodium 515mg; Carbs 2.86g; Fibre 0.9g; Sugar 0.57g; Protein 45.9g

# Seasoned Catfish Strips

**Prep time: 1 hour 15 minutes | Cook time: 20 minutes | Serves: 4**

240ml buttermilk
5 catfish fillets, cut into 4.5 cm strips
Olive oil

160g polenta
1 tablespoon cajun seasoning

1. Add the buttermilk into a shallow baking dish. Place the catfish in the dish and refrigerate for at least 1 hour to help remove any fishy taste. 2. Spray an air fryer basket lightly with olive oil. 3. In a shallow bowl, combine polenta and cajun seasoning. 4. Shake any excess buttermilk off the catfish. Place each strip in the polenta mixture and coat completely. Press the polenta into the catfish gently to help it stick. 5. Lay the strips evenly in the air fryer basket in a single layer. Lightly spray the catfish with olive oil. You may need to cook the catfish in more than one batch. 6. Air fry at 205°C for 8 minutes. Turn the catfish strips over and lightly spray with olive oil. Cook the catfish strips until they are golden brown and crispy, for 8 to 10 more minutes.

**Per Serving:** Calories 365; Fat 6.8g; Sodium 359mg; Carbs 35.4g; Fibre 1.8g; Sugar 3.8g; Protein 37.5g

# Parmesan Tuna Patty Sliders

**Prep time: 15 minutes | Cook time: 15 minutes | Serves: 4**

Olive oil
3 (125g) cans tuna, packed in water
80g whole-wheat panko bread crumbs
35g shredded Parmesan cheese

1 tablespoon sriracha
¾ teaspoon black pepper
10 whole-wheat slider buns

1. Spray an air fryer basket lightly with olive oil. 2. In a medium bowl combine the tuna, bread crumbs, Parmesan cheese, sriracha, and black pepper and stir to combine. 3. Form the mixture into 10 patties. 4. Then transfer the patties to the air fryer basket in a single layer. Spray the patties lightly with olive oil. Work in batches as needed. 5. Air fry at 175°C for 6 to 8 minutes. Turn the patties over and lightly spray with olive oil. Cook until golden brown and crisp, another 4 to 7 more minutes.
**Per Serving:** Calories 524; Fat 9.4g; Sodium 805mg; Carbs 76.6g; Fibre 7.7g; Sugar 4.7g; Protein 35.7g

# Fried Breaded Fish and Potato Chips

**Prep time: 25 minutes | Cook time: 35 minutes | Serves: 4**

**For the Chips**
1 tablespoon olive oil, plus more for spraying
2 large russet potatoes, scrubbed
**For the Fish**
Olive oil
4 (100g) cod fillets
1½ teaspoons salt, divided plus more as needed
1½ teaspoons black pepper, divided, plus more as needed

1 teaspoon salt
½ teaspoon freshly ground black pepper

65g whole-wheat flour
2 eggs
155g whole-wheat panko bread crumbs
¼ teaspoon cayenne pepper

**To make the chips:** 1. Spray an air fryer basket lightly with olive oil. 2. Cut the potatoes lengthwise into 1 cm-thick slices and then into 1 cm-thick fries. 3. In a large bowl, mix together the oil, salt, and pepper and toss with the potatoes to coat. 4. Place the potatoes in a single layer in the air fryer basket. You may need to cook them in batches. 5. Air fry at 205°C for 5 minutes. Shake the basket and cook until the potatoes are lightly browned and crisp, for 5 to 10 more minutes. Set aside and keep warm.
**To make the fish:** 1. Spray the air fryer basket with olive oil. 2. Season the fillets with salt and black pepper. 3. In a shallow bowl, mix together the whole-wheat flour, ½ teaspoon of salt, and ½ teaspoon of black pepper. 4. In a second bowl, whisk together the eggs, 1 teaspoon of water, and a pinch of salt and pepper. 5. In another shallow bowl, combine the panko bread crumbs, cayenne pepper, and remaining 1 teaspoon of salt and 1 teaspoon of black pepper. Coat each fillet in the seasoned flour, then coat with the egg, and dredge in the panko bread crumb mixture. 6. Place the fillets in the air fryer basket in a single layer. Lightly spray the fish with olive oil. You may need to cook them in batches. 7. Air fry at 205°C for 8 to 10 minutes. Turn the fillets over and lightly spray with olive oil. Cook until golden brown and crispy, for 5 to 10 more minutes.
**Per Serving:** Calories 694; Fat 22.2g; Sodium 1912mg; Carbs 90.2g; Fibre 10.8g; Sugar 2.2g; Protein 34.6g

# Mayo Salmon Burgers

**Prep time: 40 minutes | Cook time: 15 minutes | Serves: 4**

Olive oil
4 (125g) cans pink salmon in water, any skin and bones removed, drained
2 eggs, beaten
100g whole-wheat bread crumbs

4 tablespoons light mayonnaise
2 teaspoons Cajun seasoning
2 teaspoons dry mustard
4 whole-wheat buns

1. Spray an air fryer basket lightly with olive oil. 2. Mix the salmon, egg, bread crumbs, mayonnaise, Cajun seasoning, and dry mustard in a medium bowl. Cover with plastic wrap and then let it marinate in the refrigerator for 30 minutes. 3. Shape the mixture into four 1 cm thick patties about the same size as the buns. 4. Place the salmon patties in the fryer basket in a single layer and lightly spray the tops with olive oil. Cook them in batches as needed. 5. Air fry the patties at 180°C for 6 to 8 minutes. Turn the patties over and lightly spray with olive oil. Cook until crispy on the outside, for 4 to 7 more minutes. 6. Serve on whole-wheat buns.
**Per Serving:** Calories 824; Fat 42g; Sodium 1355mg; Carbs 53.3g; Fibre 2.4g; Sugar 19.1g; Protein 55.6g

# Crab Legs with Lemon Butter Dip

**Prep Time: 5 minutes | Cook Time: 15 minutes | Serves: 4**

55g salted butter, melted and divided
1.3kg crab legs

¼ teaspoon garlic powder
Juice of ½ medium lemon

1. Drizzle the crab legs with 2 tablespoons of butter, and then place the crab legs into the air fryer basket. 2. Cook the crab legs at 205°C for 15 minutes, tossing them halfway through. 3. While cooking the crab legs, mix the garlic powder, lemon juice, and the remaining butter in a small bowl. 4. Crack open crab legs, remove the meat, and dip in lemon butter to enjoy.
**Per Serving:** Calories 393; Fat 9.25g; Sodium 1862mg; Carbs 2.8g; Fibre 51.6g; Sugar 21.42g; Protein 26.06g

# Foil-Packet Lobster Tail with Parsley

**Prep Time: 15 minutes | Cook Time: 12 minutes | Serves: 2**

2 (150g) lobster tails, halved
2 tablespoons salted butter, melted

Juice of ½ medium lemon
1 teaspoon dried parsley

1. Place the two halved tails on a sheet of aluminum foil, and drizzle them with butter, and lemon juice. 2. Seal the foil packets, covering the tails completely, and then place them in the air fryer basket. 3. Cook the tails at 190°C for 12 minutes. 4. After cooking, sprinkle the tails with dried parsley, and serve immediately.
**Per Serving:** Calories 136; Fat 8.31g; Sodium 422mg; Carbs 0.99g; Fibre 0.1g; Sugar 0.31g; Protein 26.06g

# Caramelized Salmon

**Prep time: 1 hour 10 minutes | Cook time: 16 minutes | Serves: 4**

3 tablespoons soy sauce
1 tablespoon rice wine or dry sherry
1 tablespoon brown sugar
1 tablespoon toasted sesame oil
1 teaspoon minced garlic

¼ teaspoon minced ginger
4 (150g) salmon fillets, skin-on
Olive oil
½ tablespoon sesame seeds

1. Mix the soy sauce, rice wine, brown sugar, toasted sesame oil, garlic, and ginger in a small bowl. 2. Add the salmon fillets in a shallow baking dish and pour the marinade over the fillets. Cover the baking dish and let it refrigerate for at least 1 hour, turning the fillets occasionally to coat in the marinade. 3. Spray an air fryer basket lightly with olive oil. 4. Shake off any marinate and place the fillets, skin side down, in the air fryer basket in a single layer. Reserve the marinade. Work in batches as needed. 5. Air fry the fillets at 185°C for 8 to 10 minutes. Brush the tops of the salmon fillets with the reserved marinade and sprinkle with sesame seeds. 6. Increase the air fryer temperature setting to 205°C and cook for 2 to 5 more minutes for medium, 1 to 3 minutes for medium rare, or 4 to 6 minutes for well done.
**Per Serving:** Calories 341; Fat 18.4g; Sodium 919mg; Carbs 5.6g; Fibre 0.4g; Sugar 4.5g; Protein 36.2g

# Breaded Salmon Patty Bites

**Prep time: 15 minutes | Cook time: 15 minutes | Serves: 4**

Olive oil
4 (125g) cans pink salmon, skinless, boneless in water, drained
2 eggs, beaten

105g whole-wheat panko bread crumbs
4 tablespoons finely minced red pepper
2 tablespoons parsley flakes

1. Spray an air fryer basket lightly with olive oil. 2. Mix together the salmon, eggs, panko bread crumbs, red pepper, parsley flakes, and Old Bay seasoning in a medium bowl. 3. Form the mixture into 20 balls with a small cookie scoop. 4. Place the salmon bites in the air fryer basket in a single layer and spray lightly with olive oil. Work in batches as needed. 5. Air fry at 180°C until crispy for 10 to 15 minutes, shaking the basket a couple of times for even cooking.
**Per Serving:** Calories 375; Fat 13.8g; Sodium 847mg; Carbs 24.2g; Fibre 2g; Sugar 4g; Protein 36.6g

# Chapter 4 Poultry Recipes

# Italian Chicken Thighs

**Prep Time: 5 minutes | Cook Time: 20 minutes | Serves: 2**

4 bone-in, skin-on chicken thighs
2 tablespoons unsalted butter, melted
1 teaspoon dried parsley
1 teaspoon dried basil

½ teaspoon garlic powder
¼ teaspoon onion powder
¼ teaspoon dried oregano

1. Brush the unsaltedd butter over chicken thighs and sprinkle the dried parsley, basil, garlic powder, onion powder, and the dried oregano over the thighs. Place thighs into the air fryer basket. 2. Adjust the temperature setting to 195°C and set the timer for 20 minutes. 3. Halfway through the cooking time, flip the thighs. 4. When fully cooked, internal temperature will be at least 75°C and skin will be crispy. Serve warm.
**Per Serving:** Calories 493; Fat 39.14 g; Sodium 159 mg; Carbs 1.6 g; Fibre 0.3 g; Sugar 0.06 g; Protein 31.96 g

# Chicken Fajitas

**Prep Time: 10 minutes | Cook Time: 10 to 14 minutes | Serves: 4**

Cooking oil spray
4 boneless, skinless chicken breasts, sliced crosswise
1 small red onion, sliced
2 red peppers, seeded and sliced
120 ml spicy ranch salad dressing, divided

½ teaspoon dried oregano
8 corn tortillas
70 g torn butter lettuce leaves
2 avocados, peeled, pitted, and chopped

1. Insert the crisper plate into the basket and the basket into the unit. Preheat the unit by selecting BAKE, setting the temperature to 190°C, and setting the time to 3 minutes. Select START/STOP to begin. 2. Once the unit is preheated, spray the crisper plate with cooking oil. Place the chicken, red onion, and red pepper into the basket. Drizzle with 1 tablespoon of the salad dressing and season with the oregano. Toss to combine. 3. Select BAKE, set the temperature to 190°C, and set the time to 14 minutes. Select START/STOP to begin. 4. After 10 minutes, check the chicken. If a food thermometer inserted into the chicken registers at least 75°C, it is done. If not, resume cooking. 5. When the cooking is complete, transfer the chicken and vegetables to a bowl and toss with the remaining salad dressing. 6. Serve the chicken mixture family-style with the tortillas, lettuce, and avocados, and let everyone make their own plates.
**Per Serving:** Calories 919; Fat 42.05 g; Sodium 1070 mg; Carbs 62.72 g; Fibre 10.1 g; Sugar 7.41 g; Protein 72.06 g

# Chicken and Spinach Salad

**Prep Time: 10 minutes | Cook Time: 20 minutes | Serves: 4**

3 (125 g) boneless, skinless chicken breasts, cut into 2.5 cm cubes
5 teaspoons extra-virgin olive oil
½ teaspoon dried thyme
1 medium red onion, sliced

1 red pepper, sliced
1 small courgette, cut into strips
3 tablespoons freshly squeezed lemon juice
180 g fresh baby spinach leaves

1. Insert the crisper plate into the basket and the basket into the unit. Preheat the unit by selecting AIR ROAST, setting the temperature to 190°C, and setting the time to 3 minutes. Select START/STOP to begin. 2. Combine the chicken, olive oil, and thyme in a large bowl. Toss to coat. Transfer to a medium metal bowl that fits into the basket. 3. Once the unit is preheated, place the bowl into the basket. 4. Select AIR ROAST, set the temperature to 190°C, and set the time to 20 minutes. Select START/STOP to begin. 5. After 8 minutes, add the red onion, red pepper, and courgette to the bowl. Resume cooking. After about 6 minutes more, stir the chicken and vegetables. Resume cooking. 6. When the cooking is complete, a food thermometer inserted into the chicken should register at least 75°C. Remove the bowl from the unit and stir in the lemon juice. 7. Put the spinach in a serving bowl and top with the chicken mixture. Toss to combine and serve immediately.
**Per Serving:** Calories 102; Fat 5.97 g; Sodium 108 mg; Carbs 3.73 g; Fibre 1.3 g; Sugar 1.17 g; Protein 9.06 g

# Marinara Chicken with Cheeses

### Prep Time: 10 minutes | Cook Time: 20 minutes | Serves: 4

2 (100 g) boneless, skinless chicken breasts
2 egg whites, beaten
110 g Italian bread crumbs
50 g grated Parmesan cheese
2 teaspoons Italian seasoning

Salt
Freshly ground black pepper
Cooking oil spray
200 g marinara sauce
55 g shredded mozzarella cheese

1. Cut the boneless and skinless chicken breasts in half horizontally to create 4 thin cutlets on a cutting board with a knife blade parallel. On a solid surface, pound the cutlets to flatten them with your hands, a rolling pin, a kitchen mallet, or a meat hammer. 2. Pour the egg whites into a bowl large enough to dip the chicken. 3. In another bowl large enough to dip a chicken cutlet in, stir together the bread crumbs, Parmesan cheese, and Italian seasoning, and season with salt and pepper. 4. Dip each cutlet into the egg whites and into the breadcrumb mixture to coat. 5. Insert the crisper plate into the basket and the basket into the unit. Preheat the unit by selecting AIR FRY, setting the temperature to 190°C, and setting the time to 3 minutes. Select START/STOP to begin. 6. Once the unit is preheated, spray the crisper plate with cooking oil. Working in batches, place 2 chicken cutlets into the basket. Spray the chicken with cooking oil. 7. Select AIR FRY, set the temperature to 190°C, and set the time to 7 minutes. Select START/STOP to begin. 8. When the cooking is complete, repeat steps 6 and 7 with the remaining cutlets. 9. Top the chicken cutlets with the marinara sauce and shredded mozzarella cheese. If the chicken will fit into the basket without stacking, you can prepare all 4 at once. Otherwise, do these 2 cutlets at a time. 10. Select AIR FRY, set the temperature to 190°C, and set the time to 3 minutes. Select START/STOP to begin. 11. The cooking is complete when the cheese is melted and the chicken reaches an internal temperature of 75°C. Cool for 5 minutes before serving.
**Per Serving:** Calories 192; Fat 8.26 g; Sodium 574 mg; Carbs 11.41 g; Fibre 1.6 g; Sugar 3.64 g; Protein 17.26 g

# Ranch Chicken Wings

### Prep Time: 10 minutes, plus 30 minutes to marinate | Cook Time: 40 minutes | Serves: 4

2 tablespoons water
2 tablespoons hot pepper sauce
2 tablespoons unsalted butter, melted
2 tablespoons apple cider vinegar

1 (25 g) envelope ranch salad dressing mix
1 teaspoon paprika
1.8 kg chicken wings, tips removed
Cooking oil spray

1. In a large bowl, whisk the water, hot pepper sauce, melted butter, vinegar, salad dressing mix, and paprika until combined. 2. Add the wings and toss to coat. Then cover the bowl and marinate the wings in the refrigerator for 4 to 24 hours for best results. However, you can just let the wings stand for 30 minutes in the refrigerator. 3. Insert the crisper plate into the air fryer basket and the air fryer basket into the unit. Preheat the air fryer by selecting AIR FRY, setting the temperature to 205°C, and setting the timer to 3 minutes. 4. Once the unit is preheated, spray the crisper plate with cooking oil. Working in batches, put half the wings into the basket; it is okay to stack them. Refrigerate the remaining wings. 5. Select AIR FRY, set the temperature to 205°C, and set the time to 20 minutes. Select START/STOP to begin. 6. Remove and shake the air fryer basket every 5 minutes, three more times, until the chicken is browned and glazed and a food thermometer inserted into the wings registers 75°C. 7. Repeat the cooking steps with the remaining wings. 8. When the cooking is complete, serve warm.
**Per Serving:** Calories 660; Fat 24.5 g; Sodium 440 mg; Carbs 2.94 g; Fibre 0.5 g; Sugar 1.59 g; Protein 100.52 g

# Spiced Chicken Drumsticks

### Prep time: 12 minutes | Cook time: 22 minutes | Serves: 3

3 chicken drumsticks
2 tablespoons sesame oil
Salt and ground black pepper,

1 tablespoon soy sauce
1 teaspoon Five-spice powder

1. Pat the chicken drumsticks dry with paper towels. 2. Toss the chicken drumsticks with the remaining ingredients. 3. Cook the chicken drumsticks at 190°C for 22 minutes, turning them over halfway through the cooking time. Bon appétit!
**Per Serving:** Calories 321; Fat 7.9g; Sodium 789mg; Carbs 741g; Fibre 87g; Sugar 29g; Protein 93g

# Cheese & Spinach Stuffed Chicken

## Prep time: 12 minutes | Cook time: 20 minutes | Serves: 4

455 g chicken breasts, skinless, boneless and cut into pieces
2 tablespoons olives, chopped
1 garlic clove, minced
60 g spinach, torn into pieces

50 g feta cheese
Sea salt and ground black pepper,
2 tablespoons olive oil

1. Flatten the chicken breasts with a mallet. Stuff each piece of chicken with olives, garlic, spinach, and cheese. Roll them up and secure with toothpicks. 2. Spread the chicken with the salt, black pepper, and olive oil. 3. Place the stuffed chicken breasts in the Air Fryer cooking basket. Cook the chicken at 205°C for about 20 minutes, turning them over halfway through the cooking time. Bon appétit!
**Per Serving:** Calories 254; Fat 7.9g; Sodium 2544mg; Carbs 2g; Fibre 10g; Sugar 6g; Protein 11g

# Herbed Sriracha Turkey

## Prep time: 30 minutes | Cook time: 60 minutes | Serves: 5

900 g turkey breasts, rib bones trimmed
4 tablespoons butter, melted
1 teaspoon Sriracha sauce
1 tablespoon fresh coriander, chopped

1 tablespoon fresh parsley, chopped
1 tablespoon fresh thyme, chopped
Salt and freshly ground black pepper

1. Pat the turkey breasts dry with paper towels. Toss the turkey breasts with the remaining ingredients. 2. Cook the turkey breasts at 175°C for 1 hour, turning them over every 20 minutes. Bon appétit!
**Per Serving:** Calories222; Fat 7g; Sodium 634mg; Carbs 9g; Fibre 85g; Sugar 78g; Protein 32g

# Sweet and Spicy General Tso's Chicken

## Prep Time: 10 minutes | Cook Time: 14 minutes | Serves: 4

1 tablespoon sesame oil
1 teaspoon minced garlic
½ teaspoon ground ginger
240 ml chicken stock
4 tablespoons soy sauce, divided
½ teaspoon sriracha, plus more for serving

2 tablespoons hoisin sauce
4 tablespoons cornflour, divided
4 boneless, skinless chicken breasts, cut into 2.5 cm pieces
Olive oil spray
2 medium spring onions, sliced, green parts only
Sesame seeds, for garnish

1. Set a suitable saucepan over low heat, combine the sesame oil, garlic, and ginger and cook for 1 minute. 2. Add the chicken stock, 2 tablespoons of soy sauce, the sriracha, and hoisin sauce. Whisk to combine. 3. Whisk in 2 tablespoons of cornflour and continue cooking over low heat until the sauce starts to thicken, about 5 minutes. Remove the pan from heat, cover, and then set aside. 4. Insert the crisper plate into the basket and the basket into the unit. Preheat the unit by selecting BAKE, setting the temperature 205°C, and setting the time to 3 minutes. Select START/STOP to begin. 5. Toss together the chicken, remaining 2 tablespoons of soy sauce, and remaining 2 tablespoons of cornflour in a medium bowl. 6. Once the unit is preheated, spray the crisper plate with olive oil. Place the chicken into the basket and spray it with olive oil. 7. Select BAKE, set the temperature to 205°C, and set the time to 9 minutes. Select START/STOP to begin. 8. After 5 minutes, remove the basket, shake, and spray the chicken with more olive oil. Reinsert the basket to resume cooking. 9. When the cooking is up, a food thermometer inserted into the chicken should register at least 75°C. Transfer the chicken breasts to a large bowl and toss it with the sauce. Garnish with the spring onions and sesame seeds and serve.
**Per Serving:** Calories 308; Fat 11.62 g; Sodium 680 mg; Carbs 16.06 g; Fibre 0.9 g; Sugar 5.72 g; Protein 32.7 g

# Spicy Ranch Chicken Drumsticks

**Prep time: 12 minutes | Cook time: 20 minutes | Serves: 4**

60 g plain flour
1 tablespoon Ranch spicing mix
455 g chicken drumsticks

1 tablespoon hot sauce
Sea salt and ground black pepper

1. Pat the chicken drumsticks dry with paper towels. Toss the chicken drumsticks with the remaining ingredients. 2. Cook the chicken drumsticks at 190°C for 20 minutes, turning them over halfway through the cooking time. Bon appétit!
**Per Serving:** Calories 458; Fat 7.9g; Sodium 258mg; Carbs 8g; Fibre 64g; Sugar 14g; Protein 78g

# Spiced Duck Roast

**Prep time: 22 minutes | Cook time: 30 minutes | Serves: 5**

900 g duck breasts
1 tablespoon butter, melted
2 tablespoons pomegranate molasses
2 tablespoons miso paste

1 teaspoon garlic, minced
1 teaspoon ginger, peeled and minced
1 teaspoon Five-spice powder

1. Pat the duck breasts dry with paper towels. Toss the duck breast with the remaining ingredients. 2. Cook the duck breasts at 165°C for 15 minutes, turning them over halfway through the cooking time. 3. Turn the heat to 175°C; continue to cook for about 15 minutes or until cooked through. 4. Let it rest for 10 minutes before carving and serving. Bon appétit!
**Per Serving:** Calories 458; Fat 7.9g; Sodium 258mg; Carbs 8g; Fibre 64g; Sugar 14g; Protein 78g

# Sicilian Roasted Chicken

**Prep time: 10 minutes | Cook time: 12 minutes | Serves: 4**

675 g chicken fillets
2 tablespoons olive oil
1 teaspoon smoked paprika

1 teaspoon Italian spicing mix
Sea salt and ground black pepper,
50 g Pecorino Romano cheese, grated

1. Pat the chicken fillets dry with paper towels. Toss the chicken fillets with the olive oil and spices. 2. Cook the chicken fillets at 195°C for 12 minutes, turning them over halfway through the cooking time. 3. Top the chicken fillets with grated cheese and serve warm. Bon appétit!
**Per Serving:** Calories 789; Fat 7.9g; Sodium 412mg; Carbs 2g; Fibre 69g; Sugar 47g; Protein 12g

# Turkey Taquitos with Salsa

**Prep time: 15 minutes | Cook time: 25 minutes | Serves: 6**

455 g turkey breasts, boneless and skinless
Salt and freshly ground black pepper,
1 clove garlic, minced
1 habanero pepper, minced

100 g Mexican cheese blend, shredded
6 small corn tortillas
125 g salsa

1. Pat the turkey breasts dry with kitchen towels. Toss the turkey breasts with the salt and black pepper. 2. Cook the turkey breasts at 195°C for 18 minutes, turning them over halfway through the cooking time. 3. Place the shredded chicken, garlic, habanero pepper, and cheese on one end of each tortilla. Roll them up tightly and transfer them to a lightly oiled Air Fryer basket. 4. Cook your taquitos at 180°Cfor 6 minutes. Serve your taquitos with salsa and enjoy!
**Per Serving:** Calories 321; Fat 7.9g; Sodium 789mg; Carbs 741g; Fibre 87g; Sugar 29g; Protein 93g

# Crispy Chicken Nuggets

**Prep time: 10 minutes | Cook time: 12 minutes | Serves: 4**

1 egg, mixed
30 g plain flour
100 g spiced breadcrumbs

1 tablespoon olive oil
Sea salt and ground black pepper,
675 g chicken breasts, cut into small pieces

1. Mix the egg and flour in a bowl. In a separate bowl, mix the breadcrumbs, olive oil, salt, and black pepper. 2. Dip the chicken breasts into the egg mixture. Then, roll the chicken breasts over the breadcrumb mixture. 3. Cook the chicken at 195°C for 12 minutes, turning them over halfway through the cooking time. Bon appétit!
**Per Serving:** Calories 254; Fat 7.9g; Sodium 2544mg; Carbs 2g; Fibre 10g; Sugar 6g; Protein 11g

# Sweet and Sour Chicken Wings

**Prep time: 15 minutes | Cook time: 12 minutes | Serves: 6**

16 winglets
½ teaspoon sea salt
2 tablespoon light soy sauce
¼ teaspoon white pepper powder

½ crush black pepper
2 tablespoon honey
2 tablespoon lime juice

1. Place all of the ingredients in a glass dish. Coat the winglets well and allow to marinate in the refrigerator for a minimum of 6 hours. Allow to return to room temperature for 30 minutes. 2. Put the wings in the Air Fryer and air fry at 180°C for 6 minutes. Turn each wing over before cooking for another 6 minutes. Allow the chicken to cool before serving with lemon wedges.
**Per Serving:** Calories222; Fat 7g; Sodium 634mg; Carbs 9g; Fibre 85g; Sugar 78g; Protein 32g

# Dijon-Glazed Chicken Sausage

**Prep time: 10 minutes | Cook time: 20 minutes | Serves: 4**

1 tablespoon balsamic vinegar
4 chicken sausages
60g mayonnaise

2 tablespoons Dijon mustard
½ teaspoon dried rosemary

1. Place the sausages in the Air Fryer after arranging them on the grill pan. 2. The sausages should be grilled for around 13 minutes at 175°C. Halfway through cooking, turn them. 3. In the interim, make the sauce by whisking the remaining ingredients together. 4. Serve cooled Dijon sauce beside the warm sausages. Enjoy!
**Per Serving:** Calories 129, Fat 10.18g; Sodium 454mg; Carbs 4.4g; Fibre 1.3g; Sugar 0.8g; Protein 6.46g

# Crispy Chicken Tenderloins

**Prep time: 15 minutes | Cook time: 12 minutes | Serves: 6**

8 chicken tenderloins
1 egg, beaten
2 tablespoons olive oil

100 g bread crumbs
Pepper and salt

1. Pre-heat the Air Fryer to 175°C. Combine the friendly bread crumbs, olive oil, pepper, and salt in a dish. 2. Put the beaten egg in separate dish. Dip the chicken tenderloins into the egg before rolling them in the bread crumbs. 3. Transfer to the Air Fryer basket. Air fry the chicken for 12 minutes.
**Per Serving:** Calories 789; Fat 7.9g; Sodium 412mg; Carbs 2g; Fibre 69g; Sugar 47g; Protein 12g

# Chicken Veggie Kebabs

**Prep time: 15 minutes | Cook time: 15 minutes | Serves: 6**

455 g chicken breasts, diced
5 tablespoon honey
120 ml soy sauce
6 large mushrooms, cut in halves
3 medium peppers, cut

1 small courgette, cut into rings
2 medium tomatoes, cut into rings
Salt and pepper
30 g sesame seeds
1 tablespoon olive oil

1. Cube the chicken breasts and place them in a bowl. 2. Spice with some salt and pepper. Drizzle over one tablespoon of olive oil and mix well. Pour in the honey and soy sauce, and add in the sesame seeds. Leave to marinate for 15 – 30 minutes. 3. Slice up the vegetables. Thread the chicken and vegetables on wooden skewers, in alternating patterns. 4. Pre-heat the Air Fryer to 170°C. Put the chicken kebabs into the fryer basket. Cook for about 15 minutes, flipping once during cooking. Serve once crispy and brown.
**Per Serving:** Calories222; Fat 7g; Sodium 634mg; Carbs 9g; Fibre 85g; Sugar 78g; Protein 32g

# Piri Piri Chicken Wings

**Prep time: 10 minutes | Cook time: 90 minutes | Serves: 6**

35g butter, melted
1 teaspoon garlic paste
12 chicken wings
**For the Sauce**
⅓ teaspoon sea salt
½ teaspoon tarragon
50g piri piri peppers, stemmed and chopped

1 teaspoon onion powder
½ teaspoon cumin powder

1 tablespoon pimiento, deveined and minced
1 garlic clove, chopped
2 tablespoons fresh lemon juice

1. Use a steamer basket over a saucepan of boiling water to steam the chicken wings; then turn down the heat. 2. The wings should now be steam-cooked for ten minutes over a moderate heat. Butter, onion powder, cumin powder, and garlic paste should be mixed with the wings. 3.The chicken wings should be allowed to reach room temperature. After that, chill them for 45 to 50 minutes. 4. Make care to rotate them halfway through roasting in the preheated Air Fryer at 165°C for 25 to 30 minutes. 5. Prepare the sauce by combining all of the sauce's components in a food processor while the chicken wings are cooking. Add the prepared Piri Piri Sauce to the wings before serving.
**Per Serving:** Calories 132, Fat 7.88g; Sodium 223mg; Carbs 1.9g; Fibre 0.3g; Sugar 0.65g; Protein 13.16g

# Chicken Cordon Bleu with Ham and Cheese

**Prep time: 15 minutes | Cook time: 20 minutes | Serves: 4**

Oil, for spraying
2 (200g) boneless, skinless chicken breasts
4 slices Swiss cheese
4 slices deli ham
90g plain flour

1 large egg, lightly beaten
100g bread crumbs
½ teaspoon salt
½ teaspoon freshly ground black pepper

1. Preheat the air fryer to 190°C. Prepare the air fryer basket by lining it with parchment and lightly spraying it with oil. 2. Cut each chicken breast in half through its thickness to make 4 thin cutlets. Using a meat tenderizer, pound each cutlet until it is about ¾ inch thick. 3. Top each cutlet with a cheese slice and then a ham slice. Roll up the chicken and secure with a toothpick to hold it closed. 4. Place the beaten egg, flour, and bread crumbs in three separate bowls. 5. Coat each chicken roll in the flour, dip in the egg, and dredge in the bread crumbs until evenly coated. Season with the salt and black pepper. 6. Place the chicken rolls in the prepared basket and spray with oil. You may need to work in batches, depending on the size of your air fryer. 7. Cook for 10 minutes, flip, spray with more oil, and cook until golden brown, about 10 minutes. The internal temperature shall reach 75°C and the juices run clear.
**Per Serving:** Calories 520; Fat 15.6g; Sodium 1373mg; Carbs 39g; Fibre 2g; Sugar 2.2g; Protein 52.8g

# Crispy Chicken Drumsticks with Chives

### Prep time: 10 minutes | Cook time: 30 minutes | Serves: 3

1 heaping tablespoon fresh chives, chopped
1 teaspoon garlic paste
½ teaspoon ground white pepper
1 teaspoon seasoning salt

1 whole egg + 1 egg white
6 chicken drumsticks
1 teaspoon rosemary
35g almond meal

1. Set your Air Fryer to 200°C to begin. 2. In a small bowl, combine the rosemary, garlic paste, salt, white pepper, and almond meal. 3. The eggs should be beaten till foamy in another basin. 4. The chicken should be coated with flour mixture once more after being dipped in beaten eggs and flour mixture. 5. Cook the chicken drumsticks for 22 minutes. Serve hot with chives as a garnish.
Per Serving: Calories 464, Fat 11.41g; Sodium 1107mg; Carbs 0.78g; Fibre 0.2g; Sugar 0.11g; Protein 86.3g

# Cheese Chicken Breasts in Wine Sauce

### Prep time: 10 minutes | Cook time: 35 minutes | Serves: 6

1 teaspoon freshly cracked black pepper
2 tablespoons olive oil
1 teaspoon seasoned salt
35g Parmigiano-Reggiano cheese, freshly grated
3 cloves garlic, minced

3 boneless and skinless chicken breasts, cut into small pieces
80ml cooking wine (such as Sauvignon Blanc)
1 teaspoon fresh sage leaves, minced
1 teaspoon fresh rosemary leaves, minced

1. In a sauté pan, warm the oil over a moderate temperature. The garlic should then be sautéed until just fragrant. 2. After that, turn off the heat and add the cooking wine. Once the seasonings have been added, mix everything together thoroughly. Put this mixture in a baking dish that has been lightly greased. 3. Add the chicken breast pieces and roast for 32 minutes at 160°C in the preheated Air Fryer. 4. After serving the chicken on separate dishes, top with grated cheese.
Per Serving: Calories 231, Fat 9.64g; Sodium 549mg; Carbs 1.81g; Fibre 0.2g; Sugar 0.16g; Protein 32.39g

# Ginger Chicken Thighs with Pineapple

### Prep time: 7 minutes plus 30 minutes to marinate | Cook time: 15 minutes | Serves: 4

Oil, for spraying
4 (150g) boneless, skinless chicken thighs
1 (200g) can pineapple chunks, drained, 60 ml juice reserved
60ml soy sauce

50g packed light brown sugar
2 tablespoons ketchup
1 tablespoon minced garlic
2 teaspoons ground ginger

1. Prepare the air fryer basket by lining it with parchment and lightly spraying it with oil. 2. Pierce the chicken thighs several times with a fork and place them in a zip-top plastic bag. 3. Add together the reserved pineapple juice, soy sauce, brown sugar, ketchup, garlic, and ginger in a small bowl and whisk well. 4. Pour half of the sauce into the zip-top bag with the chicken, seal, and refrigerate for at least 30 minutes. 5. Place the chicken in the prepared basket, reserving the marinade. 6. Cook at 180°C for 7 minutes, flip, and cook for another 8 minutes. When cooked, the internal temperature reaches 75°C and the juices run clear. 7. Meanwhile, in a small saucepan over medium heat, bring the marinade to a boil, then simmer to thicken, stirring frequently, for 8 to 10 minutes. 8. Top the chicken thighs with the pineapple chunks and sauce and serve.
Per Serving: Calories 456; Fat 18.4g; Sodium 1052mg; Carbs 30g; Fibre 1.3g; Sugar 26.4g; Protein 42.4g

# Peppercorns Chicken Breasts

**Prep time: 10 minutes | Cook time: 40 minutes | Serves: 4**

¾ teaspoon fine sea salt
1½ tablespoons Worcester sauce
75g of spring onions, chopped
1 Serrano pepper, deveined and chopped
1 pepper, deveined and chopped
1 tablespoon tamari sauce

480ml of roasted vegetable stock
2 chicken breasts, cut into halves
¼ teaspoon mixed peppercorns, freshly cracked
1 teaspoon cumin powder
1½ teaspoons sesame oil

1. Deep-fry the chicken breasts in the vegetable stock for 10 minutes, then turn down the heat and simmer for an additional 10 minutes. 2. After that, let the chicken cool somewhat and shred it with two forks or a stand mixer. 3. Toss the shredded chicken with the salt, cracked peppercorns, cumin, sesame oil and the Worcester sauce; air-fry them at 195°C for 18 minutes; check for doneness. 4. The remaining ingredients are prepared in the meantime over a medium flame in a nonstick frying pan. 5. The onions and peppers should be cooked until soft and aromatic. 6. After turning off the heat, add the chicken shreds and stir everything together. Serve immediately.
**Per Serving:** Calories 1229, Fat 124.5g; Sodium 613mg; Carbs 4.88g; Fibre 1.1g; Sugar 1.39g; Protein 31.79g

# Chili Chicken Fajita

**Prep time: 7 minutes | Cook time: 20 minutes | Serves: 4**

Oil, for spraying
455g boneless, skinless chicken breasts, thinly sliced
2 peppers, seeded and thinly sliced
1 onion, thinly sliced
1 tablespoon olive oil

2 teaspoons chili powder
1 teaspoon salt
1 teaspoon ground cumin
4 corn or flour tortillas, at room temperature

1. Assorted toppings, such as shredded cheese, guacamole, shredded lettuce, chopped tomato, or sour cream. 2. Line the air fryer basket with parchment and spray lightly with oil. 3. Place the chicken, peppers, onion, olive oil, chili powder, salt, and cumin in a zip-top plastic bag, seal, and shake until evenly coated. Transfer the mixture to the prepared basket. 4. Cook at 180°C for 16 to 20 minutes, stirring after 10 minutes. The internal temperature of the chicken shall reach 75°C and the juices will run clear. 5. To warm the tortillas, stack them on a microwave-safe plate with a damp paper towel between each one and microwave for 30 to 60 seconds. Spoon the chicken mixture on top and serve with toppings on the side.
**Per Serving:** Calories 380; Fat 17.3g; Sodium 1173mg; Carbs 27.3g; Fibre 3.2g; Sugar 2.8g; Protein 29g

# Cheddar Chicken with Enchilada Sauce

**Prep time: 10 minutes | Cook time: 8 minutes | Serves: 4**

Oil, for spraying
420g shredded cooked chicken
1 package taco seasoning
8 flour tortillas, at room temperature

120g canned black beans, rinsed and drained
100g shredded cheddar cheese
1 (250g) can enchilada sauce

1. Prepare the air fryer basket by lining it with parchment and lightly spraying it with oil. (The parchment will keep the sauce and cheese from dripping through the holes.) 2. Mix the chicken and taco seasoning in a small bowl. 3. Divide the mixture among the tortillas. Top with the black beans and green chilies. Carefully roll up each tortilla. 4. Place the enchiladas, seam-side down, in the prepared basket. Work in batches as needed. 5. Spoon the enchilada sauce over the enchiladas. Use just enough sauce to keep them from drying out. You can add more sauce when serving. Sprinkle the cheese on top. 6. Cook at 180°C for 5 to 8 minutes, or until heated through and the cheese is melted. 7. Place 2 enchiladas on each serving plate and top with more enchilada sauce, if desired.
**Per Serving:** Calories 838; Fat 34.3g; Sodium 1526mg; Carbs 76.8g; Fibre 9g; Sugar 6g; Protein 53.6g

# Ranch Chicken Nachos

**Prep time: 5 minutes | Cook time: 5 minutes | Serves: 8**

Oil, for spraying
420g shredded cooked chicken
1 (25g) package ranch seasoning
60g sour cream

80g corn tortilla chips
35g bacon bits
100g shredded cheddar cheese
1 tablespoon chopped spring onions

1. Prepare the air fryer basket by lining it with parchment and lightly spraying it with oil. 2. Mix the chicken, ranch seasoning, and sour cream in a small bowl. 3. Place the tortilla chips in the prepared basket and top with the chicken mixture. Add the bacon bits, cheddar cheese, and spring onions . 4. Cook at 220°C for 3 to 5 minutes, or until heated through and the cheese is melted.

**Per Serving:** Calories 254; Fat 15.4g; Sodium 377mg; Carbs 7.6g; Fibre 1g; Sugar 0g; Protein 20g

# Spicy Garlic Chicken

**Prep time: 5 minutes | Cook time: 30 minutes | Serves: 4**

Oil, for spraying
4 (150g) boneless, skinless chicken breasts
1 tablespoon olive oil
1 tablespoon paprika

1 tablespoon packed light brown sugar
½ teaspoon cayenne pepper
½ teaspoon onion powder
½ teaspoon granulated garlic

1. Line the air fryer basket with parchment and spray lightly with oil. 2. Brush the chicken with the olive oil. 3. Mix the paprika, brown sugar, cayenne pepper, onion powder, and garlic in a small bowl and sprinkle it over the chicken. 4. Place the chicken in the prepared basket. You may need to work in batches, depending on the size of your air fryer. 5. Cook the prepared chicken in your air fryer at 180°C for 15 minutes, flip, and continue cooking it until the internal temperature reaches 75°C, about 15 minutes. Serve immediately.

**Per Serving:** Calories 319; Fat 10g; Sodium 831mg; Carbs 4.8g; Fibre 1g; Sugar 3.6g; Protein 51g

# Cheese Spaghetti Pie

**Prep Time: 15 minutes | Cook Time: 22 minutes | Serves: 4**

**For Ricotta Cheese Layer**
160g ricotta cheese
1 tablespoon grated Parmesan cheese
**For Spaghetti Crust**
2 tablespoons butter, melted
1 large egg
100g grated Parmesan cheese
**For Toppings**
2 teaspoons olive oil
55g diced peeled yellow onion
50g diced seeded green pepper

½ teaspoon salt

¼ teaspoon salt
150g dry gluten-free spaghetti, cooked according to instructions

225g chicken mince
240ml marinara sauce
60g grated mozzarella cheese

1. To make the ricotta cheese layer, combine all the Ricotta Cheese Layer ingredients in a small bowl. 2. To make the spaghetti crust, mix the butter, egg, Parmesan, and salt in a large bowl; stir in the drained, cooled cooked spaghetti. Set aside. 3. To make the toppings, heat the olive oil in a medium skillet over medium heat for 30 seconds; add onion and pepper, and cook them for 3 minutes until onions are translucent; add the chicken mince, and stir-fry for 5 minutes until no longer pink. 4. Preheat the air fryer at 175°C for 3 minutes. Lightly grease the air fryer basket with cooking oil. 5. Gently press spaghetti mixture into an 18 cm spring-form pan, spread ricotta mixture evenly on top. Top with toppings mixture, followed by marinara sauce. 6. Place spring-form pan in air fryer basket, and cook for 10 minutes. 7. Spread mozzarella cheese evenly on top, and cook for an additional 4 minutes. 8. Transfer pan to a cutting board and let rest 20 minutes. Once set, release sides of spring-form pan. Slice and serve pie.

**Per Serving:** Calories 355; Fat 19.34g; Sodium 1321mg; Carbs 22.5g; Fibre 2.4g; Sugar 3.77g; Protein 23.46g

# Honey-Mustard Chicken Salad

**Prep time: 10 minutes | Cook time: 10 to 13 minutes | Serves: 4**

3 boneless, skinless chicken breasts, cut into 2.5 cm cubes
1 small red onion, sliced
1 orange pepper, sliced
4 tablespoons honey mustard salad dressing, divided

½ teaspoon dried thyme
120g mayonnaise
2 tablespoons lemon juice

1. Place the chicken, onion, pepper, and squash in the air fryer basket. Drizzle with 1 tablespoon of the honey mustard salad dressing, add the thyme, and toss. 2. Roast at 205°C for 10 to 13 minutes or until the chicken is 75°C on a food thermometer, tossing the food once during cooking time. 3. Transfer the vegetables and chicken to a bowl and mix in the remaining 3 tablespoons of honey mustard salad dressing, the mayonnaise, and lemon juice. Serve on lettuce leaves, if desired.
**Per Serving:** Calories 337; Fat 19.3g; Sodium 765mg; Carbs 9.3g; Fibre 1.6g; Sugar 4.8g; Protein 31g

# Savoury Wings

**Prep Time: 5 minutes | Cook Time: 25 minutes | Serves: 4**

900g bone-in chicken wings, separated at joints
1 teaspoon salt

½ teaspoon ground black pepper

1. Sprinkle the chicken wings with salt and pepper, then place in the air fryer basket in a single layer. 2. Cook the chicken wings at 205°C for 25 minutes until they are golden brown and have an internal temperature of at least 75°C, shaking the basket every 7 minutes during cooking. 3. Serve warm.
**Per Serving:** Calories 287; Fat 8.04g; Sodium 765mg; Carbs 0.24g; Fibre 0.1g; Sugar 0g; Protein 49.87g

# Garlic Turkey Breast with Parsley

**Prep time: 10 minutes | Cook time: 60 minutes | Serves: 4**

Oil, for spraying
1 (1.2kg) bone-in turkey breast
2 tablespoons unsalted butter, melted
½ teaspoon granulated garlic

¼ teaspoon poultry seasoning
⅛ teaspoon salt
⅛ teaspoon dried parsley

1. Preheat the air fryer to 175°C. Prepare the air fryer basket by lining it with parchment and lightly spraying it with oil. 2. Place the turkey breast in the prepared basket, breast-side up, spray with oil, and cook for 20 minutes. Flip and cook, breast-side down, for another 20 minutes. Flip again and resume cooking for 15 minutes, until the internal temperature reaches 75°C. 3. Mix together the melted butter, garlic, poultry seasoning, salt, and parsley in a small bowl. 4. Brush the butter mixture all over the turkey and cook for another 5 minutes, or until the skin is browned and crispy.
**Per Serving:** Calories 570; Fat 27.8g; Sodium 281mg; Carbs 0g; Fibre 0g; Sugar 0g; Protein 74.7g

# Pepperoni Chicken Pizza

**Prep time: 10 minutes | Cook time: 20 minutes | Serves: 4**

16 slices pepperoni
Salt and pepper, to savor
60g mozzarella cheese, shredded
1½ tablespoons dried oregano

1½ tablespoons olive oil
4 small-sized chicken breasts, boneless and skinless
60ml pizza sauce

1. Apply a rolling pin to the chicken breast and gently flatten it. 2. Divide the ingredients among four chicken fillets. Roll the chicken fillets with the stuffing and seal them using a small skewer or two toothpicks. 3. Roast in the Air Fryer grill pan that has been warmed to 185°C for or 13 to 15 minutes.
**Per Serving:** Calories 662, Fat 40.91g; Sodium 522mg; Carbs 3.16g; Fibre 0.7g; Sugar 1.5g; Protein 66.76g

# Chapter 5 Beef, Pork, and Lamb Recipes

# Breaded Pork Chops

### Prep Time: 5 minutes | Cook Time: 15 minutes | Serves: 5

5 (90 – 125 g) pork chops (bone-in or boneless)
Seasoning salt
Pepper

30 g plain flour
2 tablespoons panko bread crumbs
Cooking oil

1. Season the pork chops with the seasoning salt and pepper. 2. Sprinkle the flour on both sides of the pork chops, then coat both sides with panko bread crumbs. 3. Add the pork chops in the air fryer. It's okay to stack them. Spray the pork chops with cooking oil. Cook at 195°C for 6 minutes. 4. Open the air fryer and then flip the pork chops. Cook for an additional 6 minutes. 5. Cool before serving.

**Per Serving:** Calories 134; Fat 36g; Sodium 105mg; Carbs 2.4g; Fibre 0.8g; Sugar 1.5g; Protein 9.7g

# Italian Parmesan Breaded Pork Chops

### Prep Time: 5 minutes | Cook Time: 25 minutes | Serves: 5

5 (90 – 125 g) pork chops (bone-in or boneless)
1 teaspoon Italian seasoning
Seasoning salt
Pepper

30 g plain flour
2 tablespoons Italian bread crumbs
3 tablespoons finely grated Parmesan cheese
Cooking oil

1. Season the pork chops with the Italian seasoning, seasoning salt, and pepper. 2. Sprinkle the flour on both sides of the pork chops, then coat both sides with the bread crumbs and Parmesan cheese. 3. Add the pork chops to the air fryer. Stacking them. Spray the pork chops with cooking oil. Cook at 195°C for 6 minutes. 4. Open the air fryer and then flip the pork chops. Cook for an additional 6 minutes. 5. Cool before serving.

**Per Serving:** Calories 148; Fat 4.7g; Sodium 200mg; Carbs 15.3g; Fibre 0.9g; Sugar 1.6g; Protein 10.6g

# Air Fried Sausage, Peppers, and Onions

### Prep Time: 5 minutes | Cook Time: 15 minutes | Serves: 5

5 Italian sausages
1 green pepper, cut into strips without seeds
1 red pepper, seeded and cut into strips
½ onion, cut into strips

1 teaspoon dried oregano
½ teaspoon garlic powder
5 Italian rolls or buns

1. Place the sausages in the air fryer. Cook at 180°C for 10 minutes. 2. Season the green and red peppers and the onion with the oregano and garlic powder. 3. Open the air fryer and then flip the sausages. Add the peppers and onion to the basket. Cook them in your air fryer for an additional 3 to 5 minutes, until the vegetables are soft and the sausages are no longer pink on the inside. 4. Serve the sausages (sliced or whole) on buns with the peppers and onion.

**Per Serving:** Calories 521; Fat 37g; Sodium 1038mg; Carbs 25g; Fibre 1.5g; Sugar 4g; Protein 20.8g

# Mini Beef Meatloaves with Ketchup

### Prep time: 15 minutes | Cook time: 25 minutes | Serves: 4

455 g chuck mince
1 tablespoon olive oil
1 small-sized onion, chopped
2 garlic cloves, minced

25 g breadcrumbs
1 egg, beaten
Sea salt and ground black pepper,
120 g ketchup

1. Thoroughly combine all ingredients, except for the ketchup; mix until everything is well combined. 2. Scrape the beef mixture into a lightly oiled muffin tin and transfer it to the Air Fryer cooking basket. Cook your meatloaves at 195°C for 20 minutes. Then, spread the ketchup over the top of the meatloaves. Continue cooking for another 5 minutes. Bon appétit!

**Per Serving:** Calories 789; Fat 7.9g; Sodium 412mg; Carbs 2g; Fibre 69g; Sugar 47g; Protein 12g

# Sweet and Spicy Short Ribs

**Prep Time: 65 minutes | Cook Time: 10 minutes | Serves: 4**

8 (200 g) bone-in short ribs
120 ml soy sauce
60 ml rice wine vinegar
55 g chopped onion
2 garlic cloves, minced
1 tablespoon sesame oil

1 teaspoon Sriracha
4 spring onions, green parts (white parts optional), thinly sliced, divided
Salt
Pepper

1. Place the short ribs in a sealable plastic bag. Add soy sauce, rice wine vinegar, onion, garlic, sesame oil, Sriracha, and half of the spring onions. Season with salt and pepper. 2. Seal the plastic bag and place it in the refrigerator to marinate for at least 1 hour (overnight is optimal). 3. Place the short ribs in the air fryer. (Do not overfill. You may have to cook in two batches.) Cook for 4 minutes. 4. Open the air fryer and then flip the ribs. Cook for an additional 4 minutes. (If necessary, remove the cooked short ribs from the air fryer, then repeat steps 3 and 4 for the remaining ribs.) 5. Sprinkle the short ribs with the remaining spring onions, and serve.

**Per Serving:** Calories 258; Fat 15g; Sodium 522mg; Carbs 11g; Fibre 1.1g; Sugar 7.4g; Protein 18.5g

# Beef Taco Chimichangas

**Prep Time: 10 minutes | Cook Time: 20 minutes | Serves: 4**

Cooking oil
55 g chopped onion
2 garlic cloves, minced
455 g lean beef mince
2 tablespoons taco seasoning
Salt

Pepper
1 (375 g) can diced tomatoes with chiles
4 medium (20 cm) flour tortillas
100 g Cheddar cheese, shredded (a blend of 50 g shredded Cheddar and 50 g shredded Monterey Jack works great, too)

1. Spray a frying pan with cooking oil and turn medium-high heat on. Add chopped onion and garlic, cook for 2 to 3 minutes until fragrant. 2. Add beef mince, taco seasoning, salt, and pepper. Break up the beef with a spatula. Cook for 2 to 4 minutes until browned. 3. Add the diced tomatoes with chiles. Stir to combine. 4. Mound some of the beef mince mixture on each tortilla. 5. Fold the sides of the tortilla in toward the middle and then roll up from the bottom to form chimichangas. (You can secure the chimichanga with a toothpick. Or you can moisten the upper edge of the tortilla with a small amount of water before sealing. Use a cooking brush or dab with your fingers.) 6. Spray the chimichangas with cooking oil. Place the chimichangas in the air fryer. Do not stack. Cook in batches 205°C for 8 minutes. 7. Remove the cooked chimichangas from the air fryer and top them with the shredded cheese. The heat from the chimichangas will melt the cheese. (Repeat the steps for the remaining chimichangas) 8. Serve.

**Per Serving:** Calories 494; Fat 16g; Sodium 1552mg; Carbs 49.5g; Fibre 6.5g; Sugar 16.18g; Protein 39.2g

# Savory Worcestershire Cheeseburgers

**Prep Time: 5 minutes | Cook Time: 15 minutes | Serves: 4**

455 g lean beef mince
1 teaspoon Worcestershire sauce
1 tablespoon burger seasoning
Salt

Pepper
Cooking oil
4 slices cheese
4 buns

1. Mix the beef mince, Worcestershire, burger seasoning, salt, and pepper in a large bowl. 2. Spray the cooking oil over the air fryer basket. (only a quick spritz, the burgers will produce oil as they cook.) 3. Shape the mixture into 4 patties. Place the burgers in the air fryer. Cook at 180°C for 8 minutes. 4. Open the air fryer and then flip the burgers. Cook for an additional 3 to 4 minutes. 5. Stick a knife or fork in the centre to examine the colour to check the inside of the burgers when they are fully cooked. 6. Add one cheese slice on top of each burger. Cook in your air fryer for an additional minute, or until the cheese has melted. 7. Serve on buns with any additional toppings of your choice.

**Per Serving:** Calories 648; Fat 37g; Sodium 990mg; Carbs 37g; Fibre 1.2g; Sugar 20g; Protein 39g

# Roast Ribeye Steak with Herb Butter Sauce

### Prep time: 7 minutes | Cook time: 12 minutes | Serves: 5

900 g ribeye steaks, bone-in
Salt and freshly ground black pepper,
3 tablespoons butter
1 tablespoon fresh basil, minced

1 tablespoon fresh parsley, minced
2 tablespoons fresh spring onion s, minced
2 cloves garlic, minced
Salt and freshly ground black pepper

1. Toss the steak with the salt and black pepper; place the steak in a lightly oiled Air Fryer cooking basket. Cook the steak at 205°C for 12 minutes, turning it over halfway through the cooking time. 2. In the meantime, mix the butter with the remaining ingredients and place it in the refrigerator until well-chilled. 3. Serve the warm steak with the chilled herb butter and enjoy!
**Per Serving:** Calories 254; Fat 7.9g; Sodium 2544mg; Carbs 2g; Fibre 10g; Sugar 6g; Protein 11g

# Grilled Butter Ribeye Steak

### Prep time: 10 minutes | Cook time: 15 minutes | Serves: 5

675 g ribeye steak
Sea salt and freshly ground black pepper,
1 tablespoon olive oil

2 garlic cloves, minced
55 g butter, cold and cut into cubes

1. Toss the ribeye steak with the salt, black pepper, olive oil, and garlic; place the ribeye steak in the Air Fryer cooking basket. Cook the ribeye steak at 205°Cfor 15 minutes, turning it over halfway through the cooking time. 2. Top the ribeye steak with the butter and serve warm. Bon appétit!
**Per Serving:** Calories 321; Fat 7.9g; Sodium 789mg; Carbs 741g; Fibre 87g; Sugar 29g; Protein 93g

# Wine- Braised Chuck Roast

### Prep time: 60 minutes | Cook time: 55 minutes | Serves: 5

120 ml red wine
1 tablespoon Dijon mustard
1 tablespoon fresh garlic, minced
1 teaspoon red pepper flakes, crushed

Sea salt and ground black pepper,
900 g chuck roast
1 tablespoon corn flour

1. Place the wine, mustard, garlic, red pepper, salt, black pepper, and chuck roast in a ceramic bowl. 2. Cover the bowl and let the meat marinate for 3 hours in your refrigerator. Toss the roast beef with the corn flour; place the roast beef in the Air Fryer cooking basket. Cook the roast beef at 200°C for 55 minutes, turning them over halfway through the cooking time. Enjoy!
**Per Serving:** Calories 321; Fat 7.9g; Sodium 789mg; Carbs 741g; Fibre 87g; Sugar 29g; Protein 93g

# Spicy Chuck Eye Roast with Tomatoes

### Prep time: 20 minutes | Cook time: 45 minutes | Serves: 4

675 g chuck eye roast
Sea salt and ground black pepper,
1 teaspoon red pepper flakes, crushed

2 tablespoons olive oil, melted
1 jalapeno pepper, chopped
1 large-sized tomato, sliced

1. Toss the roast beef with the salt, black pepper, red pepper flakes, and olive oil; place the roast beef in a lightly oiled Air Fryer cooking basket. 2. Cook the roast beef at 200°C for 45 minutes, turning it over halfway through the cooking time. 3. Top the roast beef with the tomato and jalapeno pepper. Continue to cook for 10 minutes more. Enjoy!
**Per Serving:** Calories222; Fat 7g; Sodium 634mg; Carbs 9g; Fibre 85g; Sugar 78g; Protein 32g

# Delicious Beef Broccoli Patties

**Prep time: 10 minutes | Cook time: 15 minutes | Serves: 4**

455 g beef
225 g broccoli, minced
1 small onion, chopped

2 garlic cloves, minced
Sea salt and ground black pepper,
1 tablespoon tamari sauce

1. In a mixing bowl, thoroughly combine all ingredients. 2. Shape the mixture into four patties. Cook the burgers at 195°C for about 15 minutes or until cooked through; make sure to turn them over halfway through the cooking time. 3. Serve the warm patties with the topping of choice. Bon appétit!
**Per Serving:** Calories222; Fat 7g; Sodium 634mg; Carbs 9g; Fibre 85g; Sugar 78g; Protein 32g

# Sweet Glazed Corned Beef

**Prep time: 15 minutes | Cook time: 60 minutes | Serves: 4**

675 g beef brisket
2 tablespoons tomato ketchup
1 tablespoon brown mustard
1 teaspoon chili powder
2 tablespoons salt

1 teaspoon garlic powder
1 teaspoon onion powder
1 tablespoon ground black pepper
1 tablespoon brown sugar

1. Toss the beef with the remaining ingredients; place the beef in the Air Fryer cooking basket. 2. Cook the beef at 200°C for 15 minutes, turn the beef over and reduce the temperature to 180°C. Continue to cook the beef for 55 minutes more or until cooked through. Bon appétit!
**Per Serving:** Calories 458; Fat 7.9g; Sodium 258mg; Carbs 8g; Fibre 64g; Sugar 14g; Protein 78g

# Beef Empanadas with Cheeses

**Prep Time: 15 minutes | Cook Time: 25 minutes | Serves: 15**

Cooking oil
2 garlic cloves, chopped
50 g chopped green pepper
⅓ medium onion, chopped
200 g lean beef mince
1 teaspoon burger seasoning

Salt
Pepper
15 empanada wrappers
115 g shredded mozzarella cheese
100 g shredded Pepper Jack cheese
1 tablespoon butter

1. Spray a frying pan with cooking oil and turn medium-high heat on. Add garlic, green pepper, and onion. Cook for about 2 minutes until fragrant. 2. Add the beef mince to the frying pan. Season the beef with the hamburger seasoning, salt, and pepper. Use a spatula to break up the beef into small pieces. Cook the beef until browned. Drain any excess fat. 3. Lay the empanada wrappers on a flat surface. 4. Dip a basting brush in water. Glaze each empanada wrapper with a wet brush along the edges to soften the crust and make it easier to roll.) 5. Scoop 2 to 3 tablespoons of beef mixture onto each empanada wrapper. Sprinkle the mozzarella and Pepper Jack cheeses over the beef mixture. 6. Close the empanadas by folding the empanada in half. Press along and seal the edges with the back of a fork. 7. Place 7 or 8 of the empanadas in the air fryer. Spray each with cooking oil. Cook at 205°C for 8 minutes. 8. Open the air fryer and flip the empanadas. Cook for an additional 4 minutes. 9. Remove the cooked empanadas from the air fryer, then repeat the empanada-preparing steps for the remaining empanadas. 10. For added flavour, melt the butter in the microwave for 20 seconds. Use a cooking brush to spread the melted butter over the top of each. 11. Cool before serving.
**Per Serving:** Calories 176; Fat 5.3g; Sodium 314mg; Carbs 19.8g; Fibre 0.8g; Sugar 0.5g; Protein 11.5g

# Allspice Coulotte Roast

**Prep time: 10 minutes | Cook time: 55 minutes | Serves: 5**

900 g Coulotte roast
2 tablespoons butter
Salt and ground black pepper

1 teaspoon ground allspice
1 teaspoon garlic, minced

1. Toss the beef with the remaining ingredients; place the beef in the Air Fryer cooking basket. Cook the beef at 200°C for 55 minutes, turning it over halfway through the cooking time. Enjoy!
**Per Serving:** Calories 254; Fat 7.9g; Sodium 2544mg; Carbs 2g; Fibre 10g; Sugar 6g; Protein 11g

# Spicy Herbed Filet Mignon

**Prep time: 7 minutes | Cook time: 14 minutes | Serves: 5**

455 g filet mignon
Sea salt and ground black pepper, to season
1 teaspoon red pepper flakes

1 teaspoon rosemary, finely chopped
2 tablespoons olive oil

1. Toss the filet mignon with the salt, black pepper, red pepper, rosemary, and olive oil; place the filet mignon in the Air Fryer cooking basket. 2. Cook the filet mignon at 205°C for 14 minutes, turning it over halfway through the cooking time. Enjoy!
**Per Serving:** Calories222; Fat 7g; Sodium 634mg; Carbs 9g; Fibre 85g; Sugar 78g; Protein 32g

# Italian-Style Pulled Beef

**Prep time: 10 minutes | Cook time: 70 minutes | Serves: 5**

900 g beef shoulder
Salt and ground black pepper,

2 garlic cloves, minced
1 tablespoon Italian seasoning mix

1. Toss the beef shoulder with the remaining ingredients; now, place the beef shoulder in the Air Fryer cooking basket. Cook the beef shoulder at 200°C for 15 minutes, turn the beef shoulder over and reduce the temperature to 180°C. Continue to cook the beef shoulder for approximately 55 minutes or until cooked through. 2. Shred the beef shoulder with two forks and serve with toppings of choice. Bon appétit!
**Per Serving:** Calories 458; Fat 7.9g; Sodium 258mg; Carbs 8g; Fibre 64g; Sugar 14g; Protein 78g

# Lemony Pork Skewers

**Prep time: 5 minutes | Cook time: 25 minutes | Serves: 4**

Sea salt and freshly ground black pepper, to taste
2 garlic cloves, minced
2 tablespoons extra virgin olive oil
1 teaspoon oregano
½ teaspoon ground turmeric
½ teaspoon ground coriander

1 teaspoon ground cumin
60ml dry red wine
1 lemon, ½ juiced ½ wedges
900g centre cut loin chop, cut into bite-sized pieces
2 teaspoons sweet Spanish paprika

1. In a sizable ceramic dish, combine all the ingredients except for the lemon wedges. Put it in the refrigerator and let it marinade for two hours. 2. Throw away the marinade. The pork slices should now be skewered and placed in the frying basket. 3. Cook for 15 to 17 minutes at 180°C in the preheated Air Fryer, shaking the basket every 5 minutes. Work in groups. 4. Serve right away with lemon slices as a garnish.
**Per Serving:** Calories 330, Fat 11.74g; Sodium 195mg; Carbs 2.64g; Fibre 0.7g; Sugar 0.47g; Protein 50.36g

# Beef Mushroom Muffins

**Prep time: 15 minutes | Cook time: 25 minutes | Serves: 4**

455 g beef mince
1 egg, beaten
1 teaspoon Dijon mustard
Sea salt and ground black pepper,
½ onion, minced

50 g mushrooms
25 g spiced bread crumbs
1 teaspoon Italian seasoning mix
120 g ketchup

1. Thoroughly combine all ingredients, except for the ketchup; mix until everything is well combined. 2. Scrape the beef mixture into lightly oiled silicone cups and transfer them to the Air Fryer cooking basket. 3. Cook your muffins at 195°Cfor 20 minutes. Then, spread the ketchup on the top of each muffin and continue cooking for another 5 minutes. Bon appétit!
**Per Serving:** Calories 254; Fat 7.9g; Sodium 2544mg; Carbs 2g; Fibre 10g; Sugar 6g; Protein 11g

# Dijon Steak

**Prep time: 7 minutes | Cook time: 12 minutes | Serves: 4**

675 g chuck eye steak
2 tablespoons olive oil
1 teaspoon paprika

1 tablespoon Dijon mustard
Salt and ground black pepper

1. Toss the steak with the remaining ingredients; place the steak in the Air Fryer cooking basket. 2. Cook the steak at 205°Cfor 12 minutes, turning it over halfway through the cooking time. Bon appétit!
**Per Serving:** Calories 321; Fat 7.9g; Sodium 789mg; Carbs 741g; Fibre 87g; Sugar 29g; Protein 93g

# Garlic Beef Roast

**Prep time: 10 minutes | Cook time: 55 minutes | Serves: 4**

675 g eye round roast
4 cloves garlic, peeled and thinly sliced

2 tablespoons olive oil
Salt and ground black pepper

1. Pierce the beef with a sharp knife and insert the garlic slices into the holes. 2. Toss the meat with the oil, salt, and black pepper and transfer it to the Air Fryer cooking basket. 3. Cook the roast beef at 200°C for 55 minutes, turning it over halfway through the cooking time. Enjoy!
**Per Serving:** Calories 789; Fat 7.9g; Sodium 412mg; Carbs 2g; Fibre 69g; Sugar 47g; Protein 12g

# Pork Stuffed Peppers with Cheese

**Prep time: 5 minutes | Cook time: 30 minutes | Serves: 3**

½ teaspoon sea salt
½ teaspoon black pepper
1 tablespoon fish sauce
2 ripe tomatoes, pureed
75g Monterey Jack cheese, grated

1 tablespoon olive oil
3 spring onions, chopped
1 teaspoon fresh garlic, minced
3 peppers, stems and seeds removed
150g lean pork mince

1. Boil the peppers in salted water for 4 minutes. 2. Olive oil should be heated over medium heat in a nonstick frying pan. Then, cook the garlic and spring onions in a frying pan until aromatic and soft. 3. Stir in the pork mince and continue sautéing until the pork has browned; drain off the excess fat. 4. Add the salt, black pepper, fish sauce, and 1 pureed tomato; give it a good stir. 5. Divide the filling among the peppers. 6. In a baking dish that has been lightly coated with cooking oil, arrange the peppers. Surround the peppers with the remaining tomato puree. 7. Bake for 13 minutes at 195°C in the prepared Air Fryer. Add cheese shavings, then bake for an additional six minutes. 8. Enjoy warm servings!
**Per Serving:** Calories 425, Fat 25.94g; Sodium 1101mg; Carbs 9.59g; Fibre 2.2g; Sugar 5.17g; Protein 38.3g

# Pork with Green Olives & Padrón Peppers

**Prep time: 5 minutes | Cook time: 30 minutes | Serves: 4**

1 teaspoon Celtic salt
1 teaspoon paprika
1 tablespoon olive oil
1 heaped tablespoon capers, drained

8 green olives, pitted and halved
200g Padrón peppers
900g pork loin, sliced

1. Drizzle olive oil all over the Padrón peppers and cooked in an air fryer that has been warmed to 200°C for 10 minutes, occasionally flipping the peppers to ensure even cooking. 2. Then raise the heat to 180°C. 3. Salt and paprika are used to season the pork loin. Capers are added, and they are cooked for 16 minutes while being turned over halfway through. 4. Serve with the saved Padrón peppers and olives.

**Per Serving:** Calories 536, Fat 29.49g; Sodium 845mg; Carbs 5.99g; Fibre 1.3g; Sugar 2.99g; Protein 59.41g

# Meatballs with Cheese

**Prep time: 5 minutes | Cook time: 15 minutes | Serves: 4**

1 tablespoon coriander, chopped
1 teaspoon fresh mint, minced
Sea salt and ground black pepper, to taste
½ teaspoon mustard seeds
1 teaspoon fennel seeds
225g pork mince

225g beef mince
2 garlic cloves, minced
1 shallot, chopped
1 teaspoon ground cumin
120g mozzarella, sliced

1. Combine all the ingredients excluding the mozzarella in a mixing bowl. 2. Create balls out of the mixture and place them in a frying basket that has been lightly oiled. 3. The meatballs should be cooked in the preheated Air Fryer for 10 minutes at 195°C. About halfway through the cooking process, check the meatballs. 4. Add some sliced mozzarella on top and bake for three more minutes. Place everything on a lovely serving plate to serve.

**Per Serving:** Calories 343, Fat 18.39g; Sodium 289mg; Carbs 3.54g; Fibre 1.1g; Sugar 1.23g; Protein 39.24g

# Homemade Sloppy Joes

**Prep time: 5 minutes | Cook time: 45 minutes | Serves: 4**

1 pepper, chopped
455g pork mince
1 ripe medium-sized tomato, pureed
1 tablespoon poultry seasoning blend
**Keto Buns**
1 egg
45g coconut flour
80g ricotta cheese, crumbled
1½ tablespoons plain whey protein isolate

2 garlic cloves, minced
Dash ground allspice
1 tablespoon olive oil
1 shallot, chopped

80g mozzarella cheese, shredded
50g almond flour
1 teaspoon baking soda

1. Set your Air Fryer to 200°C to begin. For a short while, let the olive oil warm up. 2. The shallots should be sautéed once hot until just tender. Add the pepper and garlic; sauté for an additional 4 minutes, or until fragrant. 3. With a fork, crumble the pork mince as it cooks for an additional 5 minutes. The spices and tomato puree are added next. Cook for a further 10 minutes at 185°C. Reserve. 4. To make the keto buns, microwave the cheese for 1 minute 30 seconds, stirring twice. In the bowl of a food processor, add the cheese and pulse until smooth. Add the egg after mixing once more. 5. Blend one more after including the flour, baking soda, and plain whey protein isolate. Scrape the batter onto the middle of a cling film that has been lightly greasing. 6. Cut the dough into four pieces, shape it into a disc, and place it on a baking sheet lined with parchment paper to cool in the freezer (make sure to grease your hands). Bake at 200°C in the preheated oven for about 14 minutes. 7. Place the keto buns in the cooking basket after spooning the meat mixture into them. Cook for another 7 minutes to fully reheat.

**Per Serving:** Calories 587, Fat 39.89g; Sodium 240mg; Carbs 15.57g; Fibre 1.2g; Sugar 6.66g; Protein 40.07g

# Sherry-Braised Ribs with Grape Tomatoes

**Prep time: 5 minutes | Cook time: 35 minutes | Serves: 2**

1 rack ribs, cut in half to fit the Air Fryer
60ml sherry wine
2 tablespoons coconut aminos
1 tablespoon Dijon mustard

Sea salt and ground black pepper, to taste
150g grape tomatoes
1 teaspoon dried rosemary

1. Combine the mustard, sherry wine, coconut aminos, salt, and black pepper with the pork ribs. 2. Add the ribs to the frying basket that has been lightly oiled. Cook for 25 minutes at 185°C in the preheated Air Fryer. 3. Cook for an additional 5 minutes after flipping the ribs over and adding the tomatoes and rosemary. Serve right away.
**Per Serving:** Calories 667, Fat 46.13g; Sodium 216mg; Carbs 17.2g; Fibre 1.5g; Sugar 13.6g; Protein 44.85g

# Pork and Mushroom Cheeseburgers

**Prep time: 10 minutes | Cook time: 20 minutes | Serves: 4**

1 tablespoon rapeseed oil
1 onion, chopped
2 garlic cloves, minced
455g pork mince
225g brown mushrooms, chopped

Salt and black pepper, to taste
1 teaspoon cayenne pepper
½ teaspoon dried rosemary
½ teaspoon dried dill
4 slices Cheddar cheese

1. To begin, warm your air fryer to 185°C. 2. Combine the oil, onions, garlic, pork mince, mushrooms, salt, black pepper, cayenne pepper, rosemary, and dill in a mixing bowl until well-combined. 3. Patties made from the meat mixture should be four. 4. Frying spray should be applied to the cooking basket's base. The meatballs should be cooked for 20 minutes at 185°C in the prepared Air Fryer, turning them over halfway through. 5. Add cheese to the heated burgers before serving. Enjoy!
**Per Serving:** Calories 593, Fat 29.67g; Sodium 367mg; Carbs 49.59g; Fibre 7.4g; Sugar 4.76g; Protein 38.05g

# Pork Tenderloin with Potatoes

**Prep Time: 5 minutes | Cook Time: 25 minutes | Serves: 4**

300g potatoes, rinsed and dried
2 teaspoons olive oil
1 (455g) pork tenderloin, cut into 2.5 cm cubes
1 onion, chopped

1 red pepper, chopped
2 garlic cloves, minced
½ teaspoon dried oregano
2 tablespoons chicken stock

1. Toss the potatoes and olive oil in a medium bowl, then transfer them to the air fryer basket. 2. Roast the potatoes at 185°C for 15 minutes. 3. Mix the potatoes, pork, onion, red pepper, garlic, and oregano in a suitable bowl, and drizzle with the chicken stock. 4. Put the bowl in the air fryer basket, then roast the mixture for about 10 minutes more until the potatoes are tender and pork reaches an internal temperature of at least 60°C, shaking the basket once during cooking. 5. Serve immediately.
**Per Serving:** Calories 221; Fat 4.91g; Sodium 69mg; Carbs 17.33g; Fibre 2.4g; Sugar 2.38g; Protein 26.04g

# Paprika Pork Sirloin with Spice Salsa Sauce

**Prep time: 5 minutes | Cook time: 55 minutes | Serves: 3**

1 tablespoon smoked paprika
2 teaspoons peanut oil
675g pork sirloin

Coarse sea salt and ground black pepper, to taste
70g prepared salsa sauce

1. Set your Air Fryer to 180°C to begin. 2. Drizzle the oil all over the pork sirloin. Add paprika, black pepper, and salt to taste. 3. Cook in the preheated Air Fryer for 50 minutes. 4. With two forks, shred the roast after removing it from the Air Fryer. Add the salsa sauce and stir. Enjoy!
**Per Serving:** Calories 301, Fat 7.24g; Sodium 269mg; Carbs 4.1g; Fibre 1.4g; Sugar 1.85g; Protein 52.85g

# French Style Pork Chops

**Prep time: 5 minutes | Cook time: 12 minutes | Serves: 4**

2 tablespoons coconut aminos
455g pork loin centre rib chops, bone-in
1 teaspoon Herbes de Provence
1 tablespoon Dijon mustard

2 tablespoons French wine
Celtic salt and ground black pepper, to taste
2 tablespoons rice vinegar

1. Combine the vinegar, wine, and coconut aminos thoroughly. Add the pork and let it marinate for 1 hour in the refrigerator. 2. Add salt, black pepper, and Herbes de Provence to the pork chops. Apply mustard liberally to the pork chops. 3. Cook for 12 minutes at 200°C in the preheated Air Fryer. If desired, serve warm with mashed potatoes.
**Per Serving:** Calories 221, Fat 9.65g; Sodium 117mg; Carbs 1.72g; Fibre 0.4g; Sugar 0.91g; Protein 29.71g

# Coconut Pork Satay

**Prep Time: 15 minutes | Cook Time: 15 minutes | Serves: 4**

1 (455g) pork tenderloin, cut into 4.5 cm cubes
40g minced onion
2 garlic cloves, minced
1 jalapeño pepper, minced

2 tablespoons freshly squeezed lime juice
2 tablespoons coconut milk
2 tablespoons unsalted peanut butter
2 teaspoons curry powder

1. Combine the pork, onion, garlic, jalapeño, lime juice, coconut milk, peanut butter, and curry powder in a medium bowl. Let stand for 10 minutes at room temperature. 2. Remove the pork from the marinade, and reserve the marinade. 3. Thread the pork onto about 8 bamboo or metal skewers. 4. Grill them at 195°C for 9 to 14 minutes until they reach an internal temperature of at least 60°C, brushing once with the reserved marinade during cooking. 5. Discard any remaining marinade after cooking.
**Per Serving:** Calories 226; Fat 8.51g; Sodium 71mg; Carbs 4.74g; Fibre 1.2g; Sugar 1.84g; Protein 32.07g

# Grilled Pork Tenderloin

**Prep Time: 15 minutes | Cook Time: 9 to 11 minutes | Serves: 4**

1 tablespoon packed brown sugar
2 teaspoons espresso powder
1 teaspoon ground paprika
½ teaspoon dried marjoram

1 tablespoon honey
1 tablespoon freshly squeezed lemon juice
2 teaspoons olive oil
1 (455g) pork tenderloin

1. Mix the brown sugar, espresso powder, paprika, marjoram, honey, lemon juice, and olive oi in a small bowl. 2. Spread the honey mixture over the pork and let stand for 10 minutes at room temperature. 3. Roast the tenderloin in the air fryer at 205°C for 9 to 11 minutes until the pork registers an internal temperature of at least 60°C. 4. Slice the meat after cooking and serve hot.
**Per Serving:** Calories 174; Fat 4.81g; Sodium 62mg; Carbs 7.89g; Fibre 0.4g; Sugar 6.51g; Protein 24g

# Pork Cabbage Burgers

**Prep Time: 20 minutes | Cook Time: 9 minutes | Serves: 4**

120g Greek yogurt
2 tablespoons low-sodium mustard, divided
1 tablespoon lemon juice
20g sliced red cabbage
30g grated carrots

455g lean pork mince
½ teaspoon paprika
30g mixed baby lettuce greens
2 small tomatoes, sliced
8 small whole-wheat sandwich buns, cut in half

1. Mix the yogurt, 1 tablespoon mustard, lemon juice, cabbage, and carrots in a small bowl, and then place the bowl in refrigerator. 2. Toss the pork with the remaining mustard, and the paprika in a medium bowl, then form the mixture into 8 small patties. 3. Put the sliders in the air fryer basket. Grill them at 205°C for 7 to 9 minutes until the sliders register 75°C. 4. Assemble the burgers by placing some of the lettuce greens on a bun bottom. Top with a tomato slice, the burgers, and the cabbage mixture. Add the bun top and serve immediately.
**Per Serving:** Calories 171; Fat 4.85g; Sodium 105mg; Carbs 6.8g; Fibre 1.5g; Sugar 3.99g; Protein 26.09g

# Mustard Pork Tenderloin

**Prep Time: 10 minutes | Cook Time: 16 minutes | Serves: 4**

3 tablespoons low-sodium grainy mustard
2 teaspoons olive oil
¼ teaspoon dry mustard powder
1 (455g) pork tenderloin, silver skin and excess fat trimmed

and discarded
2 slices whole-wheat bread, crumbled
25g ground walnuts
2 tablespoons corn flour

1. Mix the mustard, olive oil, and mustard powder in a small bowl. Spread this mixture over the pork. 2. Mix the bread crumbs, walnuts, and corn flour in a plate. 3. Dip the mustard-coated pork into the crumb mixture to coat. 4. Air-fry the pork at 205°C for 12 to 16 minutes until it registers at least 60°C. 5. Slice to serve after cooking.
**Per Serving:** Calories 215; Fat 12.75g; Sodium 362mg; Carbs 0.11g; Fibre 0g; Sugar 0g; Protein 23.66g

# Pork Tenderloin with Apple Slices

**Prep Time: 10 minutes | Cook Time: 20 minutes | Serves: 4**

1 (455g) pork tenderloin, cut into 4 pieces
1 tablespoon apple butter
2 teaspoons olive oil
2 Granny Smith apples, sliced

3 celery stalks, sliced
1 onion, sliced
½ teaspoon dried marjoram
80ml apple juice

1. Rub each piece of pork with the apple butter and olive oil. 2. Mix the pork, apples, celery, onion, marjoram, and apple juice in a suitable bowl. 3. Place the bowl into the air fryer and roast the mixture at 205°C for 14 to 19 minutes until the pork reaches at least 60°C and the apples and vegetables are tender. 4. Stir them halfway through cooking. 5. Serve immediately.
**Per Serving:** Calories 260; Fat 8.37g; Sodium 78mg; Carbs 14.31g; Fibre 2.7g; Sugar 10.24g; Protein 30.3g

# Chapter 6 Snack and Starter Recipes

# Air-fryer Raspberry Brie

**Prep Time: 15 minutes | Cook Time: 15 minutes | Serves: 6**

1 tablespoon plain flour
1 puff pastry sheet, at room temperature
1 (200 g) Brie wheel, refrigerated
80 g raspberry preserves

2 tablespoons fresh raspberries
1 large egg
1 tablespoon water
Extra-virgin olive oil, for the basket

1. Preheat the air fryer to 175°C. 2. Dust your work surface with the flour, then roll out the puff pastry sheet. 3. Cut the rind off the Brie and discard it, and place the Brie in the centre of the puff pastry sheet. 4. Spread the raspberry preserves on top of the Brie, and then sprinkle the fresh raspberries on top. 5. Fold up the sides of the puff pastry around the Brie, and press the seams of the pastry together until they are closed. 6. Whisk together the egg and water in a small bowl, and brush the egg wash all over the top and sides of the puff pastry. 7. Generously spritz the air fryer basket with oil, and place the pastry-enrobed Brie in the basket. 8. Air fry at 175°C for 10 to 15 minutes, or until the pastry is golden brown and cooked through.
**Per Serving:** Calories 598; Fat 48.02g; Sodium 1075mg; Carbs 5.6g; Fibre 0.6g; Sugar 4g; Protein 36.13g

# Italian Toasted Ravioli

**Prep Time: 15 minutes | Cook Time: 10 minutes | Serves: 6**

2 large eggs
2 tablespoons milk
30 g plain flour
80 g Italian bread crumbs
35 g grated Parmesan cheese
1 teaspoon Italian seasoning

¼ teaspoon salt
¼ teaspoon freshly ground black pepper
1 (200 g) package fresh ravioli, refrigerated
Extra-virgin olive oil, for spraying
Marinara sauce, for serving (optional)

1. To prepare, heat your air fryer to 195°C. 2. Pour the milk in a small shallow bowl and whisk together with 2 eggs. Put the flour in a second small shallow bowl. Combine the bread crumbs, Parmesan cheese, Italian seasoning, salt, and pepper in a third small shallow bowl. 3. Coat each ravioli in the flour, in the egg wash, and then in the bread crumb mixture. 4. Lightly spritz the air fryer basket with oil, putting the ravioli in a single layer in the basket and lightly spraying with oil. 5. Air fry at 175°C for 4 minutes. 6. Flip the ravioli and lightly spray with oil. 7. Air fry for another 3 to 4 minutes, or until golden brown and crispy. 8. Serve it with marinara sauce, if using.
**Per Serving:** Calories 119; Fat 4.88g; Sodium 381mg; Carbs 13.43g; Fibre 1g; Sugar 1.46g; Protein 4.98g

# Crispy Crab and Cream Cheese Wontons

**Prep time: 10 minutes | Cook time: 10 minutes | Serves: 4**

100 g ⅓-less-fat cream cheese, at room temperature
60 g lump crabmeat, picked over for bits of shell
2 spring onions, chopped
2 garlic cloves, finely minced

2 teaspoons reduced-sodium soy sauce
15 wonton wrappers
1 large egg white, beaten
5 tablespoons Thai sweet chili sauce, for dipping

1. In a bowl, combine the cream cheese, crab, spring onions, garlic, and soy sauce. Mix with a fork until thoroughly combined. 2. Working with one at a time, place a wonton wrapper on a clean surface, the points facing top and bottom like a diamond. 3. Spoon 1 level tablespoon of the crab mixture onto the centre of the wrapper. Dip your finger in a bowl of water and run it along the edges of the wrapper. Take one corner of the wrapper and fold it up to the opposite corner, forming a triangle. 4. Gently press out any air between wrapper and filling and seal the edges. Set aside, repeat with the remaining wrappers and filling. 5. Brush both sides of the wontons with egg white. Preheat the air fryer to 170°C. Working in batches, arrange a single layer of the wontons in the air fryer basket. Cook for about 8 minutes, flipping halfway, until golden brown and crispy. (For a toaster oven–style air fryer, cook at 150°C; the timing remains the same.) 6. Serve hot with the chili sauce for dipping.
**Per Serving:** Calories 789; Fat 7.9g; Sodium 412mg; Carbs 2g; Fibre 69g; Sugar 47g; Protein 12g

# Baked Jalapeño Poppers

**Prep Time: 15 minutes | Cook Time: 10 minutes | Serves: 8**

8 large jalapeños
200 g cream cheese, at room temperature
55 g panko bread crumbs
50 g shredded cheese, any variety

2 teaspoons dried parsley
½ teaspoon garlic powder
Extra-virgin olive oil, for the basket

1. Preheat the air fryer to 185°C. 2. Remove the stems of the jalapeños, and then cut them in half lengthwise. 3. Carefully remove the seeds and insides to create boats. 4. Combine the cream cheese, bread crumbs, shredded cheese, parsley, and garlic powder in a medium bowl. 5. Stuff each jalapeño half with the cream cheese mixture. 6. Lightly spritz the air fryer basket with the extra-virgin olive oil, placing the poppers in a single layer in the basket. 7. Air fry at 185°C for 7 to 10 minutes, or until the cheese is bubbly and golden brown and the jalapeños have softened.

**Per Serving:** Calories 126; Fat 11.15g; Sodium 216mg; Carbs 2.57g; Fibre 0.2g; Sugar 1.17g; Protein 4.31g

# Air-fryer Egg Rolls

**Prep Time: 15 minutes | Cook Time: 10 minutes | Serves: 5**

1 (375 g) can black beans, drained and rinsed
165 g corn kernels, frozen or canned, drained
1 (100 g) can diced green chiles
195 g shredded Colby-Jack cheese
1 teaspoon paprika
1 teaspoon chili powder

1 teaspoon salt
½ teaspoon ground cumin
½ teaspoon freshly ground black pepper
1 (300 g) package egg roll wrappers
Extra-virgin olive oil, for spraying

1. To prepare, heat the air fryer to 190°C. 2. Combine the black beans, corn, green chiles, cheese, paprika, chili powder, salt, cumin, and pepper in a large bowl. 3. Place an egg roll wrapper on your work surface diagonally. 4. Put some filling onto the centre of the wrapper. 5. Fold the bottom corner over the filling and roll up snugly halfway to cover the filling. 6. Fold in both sides of the wrapper. 7. Moisten the edges of the top corner with water, roll up the rest of the way, and seal the top corner. 8. Repeat steps 2 and 3 with the remaining ingredients. 9. Lightly spray the air fryer basket with oil. 10. Place the egg rolls seam-side down in the basket, leaving at least ½ cm between each to ensure even cooking. 11. Lightly spray with oil. 12. Air fry at 190°C for 4 minutes. 13. Flip the egg rolls and lightly spray with oil. 14. Air fry the egg rolls for another 4 to 6 minutes, or until golden brown and crispy.

**Per Serving:** Calories 269; Fat 18.02g; Sodium 963mg; Carbs 13.66g; Fibre 2.7g; Sugar 1.61g; Protein 15.07g

# Cheesy Crab Mushrooms

**Prep time: 10 minutes | Cook time: 10 minutes | Serves: 8**

16 large white mushrooms
Olive oil spray
¼ teaspoon salt
150 g lump crabmeat, picked over for bits of shell
30 g freshly grated Parmesan cheese
25 g panko bread crumbs, regular or gluten-free
3 tablespoons mayonnaise

2 tablespoons chopped spring onion s
1 large egg, beaten
1 garlic clove, minced
¾ teaspoon Old Bay Spicing
1 tablespoon chopped fresh parsley
55 g shredded mozzarella cheese

1. Wipe the mushrooms with a damp paper towel to clean. Remove the stems, finely chop, and set aside. 2. Spray the mushroom caps with oil and spread with the salt. 3. In a bowl, combine the crab, Parmesan, panko, mayonnaise, chopped mushroom stems, spring onion s, egg, garlic, Old Bay, and parsley. Mound the filling (about 2 tablespoons each) onto each mushroom cap. 4. Top each with ½ tablespoon mozzarella, pressing to stick to the crab. 5. Preheat the air fryer to 180°C. Working in batches, arrange a single layer of the stuffed mushrooms in the air fryer basket. Cook for 8 to 10 minutes, until the mushrooms are soft, the crab is hot, and the cheese is golden. (For a toaster oven–style air fryer, cook at 150°C for about 10 minutes.) Serve hot.

**Per Serving:** Calories 321; Fat 7.9g; Sodium 789mg; Carbs 741g; Fibre 87g; Sugar 29g; Protein 93g

# Garlic Buffalo Chicken Meatballs
### Prep Time: 10 minutes | Cook Time: 15 minutes | Serves: 4

455 g chicken mince
55 g panko bread crumbs
1 large egg
3 tablespoons buffalo sauce, divided
2 teaspoons minced garlic

1 teaspoon dry ranch dressing mix
½ teaspoon salt
½ teaspoon freshly ground black pepper
Extra-virgin olive oil, for the basket

1. To prepare. heat the air fryer to 175°C. 2. Combine the chicken, bread crumbs, egg, 1 tablespoon buffalo sauce, garlic, ranch dressing mix, salt, and pepper in a large bowl. 3. Form the mixture into 2.5 cm meatballs, and make sure it has about 20 meatballs. 4. Lightly spray the air fryer basket with oil, and place the meatballs in a single layer in the basket. (Air fry in batches, if necessary.) 5. Air fry at 175°C for 6 minutes. 6. Then shake the basket and air fry again for another 6 to 9 minutes, or until browned and cooked through. 7. Toss with the remaining 2 tablespoons buffalo sauce before serving.
**Per Serving:** Calories 280; Fat 18.94g; Sodium 500mg; Carbs 3.76g; Fibre 0.4g; Sugar 0.88g; Protein 22.47g

# Italian Crispy Stuffed Olives
### Prep Time: 15 minutes | Cook Time: 10 minutes | Serves: 6

1 (250 g) jar garlic- or pimento-stuffed olives
30 g plain flour
1 large egg

110 g Italian seasoned panko bread crumbs
Extra-virgin olive oil, for spraying

1. Preheat the air fryer to 205°C. 2. Remove the olives from the jar and dry them completely with paper towels. 3. Add the flour to a small shallow bowl. Beat the egg in a second small shallow bowl. Put the bread crumbs in a third small shallow bowl. 4. Toss the olives in the flour. 5. Coat each olive in the beaten egg, then in the breading. 6. Lightly spray the air fryer basket with oil, place the coated olives in a single layer in the basket, and lightly spray with oil. 7. Air fry at 205°C for 6 to 8 minutes, shaking the basket gently after 2 minutes to ensure even cooking. 8. Serve it hot.
**Per Serving:** Calories 44; Fat 1.07g; Sodium 37mg; Carbs 6.98g; Fibre 0.3g; Sugar 0.36g; Protein 1.51g

# Cheese Clam
### Prep time: 10 minutes | Cook time: 10 minutes | Serves: 6

Cooking spray
2 (160 g) cans chopped clams, in clam juice
35 g panko bread crumbs, regular or gluten-free
1 medium garlic clove, minced
1 tablespoon olive oil
1 tablespoon fresh lemon juice
¼ teaspoon Tabasco sauce

½ teaspoon onion powder
¼ teaspoon dried oregano
¼ teaspoon freshly ground black pepper
⅛ teaspoon salt
½ teaspoon sweet paprika
2½ tablespoons freshly grated Parmesan cheese
2 celery stalks, cut into 5 cm pieces

1. Spray a 5½- to 6 cm round baking dish with cooking spray. Drain one of the cans of clams. 2. Place in a bowl along with the remaining can of clams (including the juice), the panko, garlic, olive oil, lemon juice, Tabasco sauce, onion powder, oregano, pepper, salt, ¼ teaspoon of the paprika, and 2 tablespoons of the Parmesan. 3. Mix well and let sit for 10 minutes. Transfer to the baking dish. Preheat the air fryer to 160°C. Place the baking dish in the air fryer basket and cook for 10 minutes. 4. Top with the remaining ¼ teaspoon paprika and ½ tablespoon Parmesan. Cook for about 8 more minutes, until golden brown on top. (For a toaster oven–style air fryer, the temperature remains the same; cook for 10 minutes, then 2 to 3 more minutes.) 5. Serve hot, with the celery for dipping.
**Per Serving:** Calories 254; Fat 7.9g; Sodium 2544mg; Carbs 2g; Fibre 10g; Sugar 6g; Protein 11g

# Cheese Pizza Pinwheels

**Prep Time: 10 minutes | Cook Time: 20 minutes | Serves: 4**

1 tablespoon flour
1 (200 g) can crescent dough, refrigerated
125 g pizza sauce

55 g mozzarella cheese
50 g shredded Parmesan cheese
Extra-virgin olive oil, for the basket

1. Preheat the air fryer to 175°C. 2. Lightly coat your work surface with flour, then roll out the sheet of crescent dough. 3. Add the pizza sauce evenly over the crescent dough all the way to the edges. 4. Sprinkle the mozzarella cheese and Parmesan cheese over top of the pizza sauce. 5. Roll up the dough into a long tube. 6. Place the rolled tube in the freezer for about 10 minutes to make cutting easier. 7. Cut the dough roll into 2.5 cm slices. 8. Lightly spray the air fryer basket with oil. 9. Place the pinwheel slices in a single layer in the basket. 10. Allow about 1 cm between each. 11. Air fry at 175°C for 5 minutes. 12. Shake the basket and air fry for another 2 to 5 minutes, or until golden brown and cooked through.
**Per Serving:** Calories 111; Fat 4.15g; Sodium 463mg; Carbs 8.95g; Fibre 1g; Sugar 1.42g; Protein 9.26g

# Tuna and Beans Wonton Cups

**Prep time: 10 minutes | Cook time: 10 minutes | Serves: 2**

12 wonton wrappers
Olive oil spray
135 g dried beans (for weighting the cups)
2 tablespoons reduced-sodium soy sauce
1 teaspoon toasted sesame oil
½ teaspoon Sriracha sauce

115 g fresh sushi-grade ahi tuna, cut into 1 cm cubes
30 g peeled, seeded, and diced cucumber
50 g Hass avocado (about ½ small), cut into 1 cm cubes
35 g sliced spring onions
1½ teaspoons toasted sesame seeds

1. Place each wonton wrapper in a lined foil baking cup, pressing gently in the middle and against the sides to create a bowl. 2. Spray each lightly with oil. Add 1 heaping tablespoon of dried beans to the middle of each cup (this helps weight down the wrapper and keep the wontons in place during cooking). 3. Preheat the air fryer to 140°C. Working in batches, arrange a single layer of the cups in the air fryer basket. Cook for 8 to 10 minutes, until browned and crispy. (For a toaster oven–style air fryer, cook at 120°C; the timing remains the same.) 4. Carefully remove the cups and let cool slightly. Remove the beans and set the cups aside. 5. Meanwhile, in a bowl, combine the soy sauce, sesame oil, and Sriracha. Mix well to combine. 6. Add the tuna, cucumber, avocado, and spring onion s and toss gently to combine. Add 2 heaping tablespoons of the ahi mixture to each cup and top each with ⅛ teaspoon sesame seeds. 7. Serve immediately.
**Per Serving:** Calories222; Fat 7g; Sodium 634mg; Carbs 9g; Fibre 85g; Sugar 78g; Protein 32g

# Crunchy Chips with Salsa

**Prep time: 10 minutes | Cook time: 10 minutes | Serves: 4**

**Salsa**
¼ small onion
2 small garlic cloves
½ jalapeño, seeds and membranes removed
1 (365 g) can diced tomatoes, undrained
**Chips**
6 corn tortillas
Olive oil spray

Handful of fresh coriander
Juice of 1 lime
¼ teaspoon salt

¾ teaspoon chili-lime Spicing salt (such as Tajín or Trader Joe's)

1. For the salsa: In a food processor, combine the onion, garlic, jalapeño, tomatoes (including the juices), coriander, lime juice, and salt. Pulse a few times until combined and chunky (don't overprocess). Transfer to a serving bowl. 2. For the chips: Spray both sides of the tortillas with oil. Stack the tortillas on top of each other so they line up. Using a large sharp knife, cut them in half, then in litreers, and once more so they are divided into 8 equal wedges each (48 total). 3. Spread out on a work surface and spice both sides with chile-lime salt. 4. Preheat the air fryer to 205°C. Working in batches, arrange a single layer of the tortilla wedges in the air fryer basket. Cook for 5 to 6 minutes, shaking the basket halfway, until golden and crisp (be careful not to burn them). (For a toaster oven–style air fryer, cook at 175°C for 4 to 5 minutes.) 5. Let cool a few minutes before serving with the salsa.
**Per Serving:** Calories222; Fat 7g; Sodium 634mg; Carbs 9g; Fibre 85g; Sugar 78g; Protein 32g

# Tangy Tomatillo Salsa Verde

**Prep time: 10 minutes | Cook time: 25 minutes | Serves: 5**

1 large poblano pepper
1 large jalapeño
¼ small onion
2 garlic cloves
Olive oil spray

340 g tomatillos (husks removed)
3 tablespoons chopped fresh coriander
¼ teaspoon sugar (omit for keto diets)
1 teaspoon salt

1. Preheat the air fryer to 205°C. Spritz the poblano, jalapeño, onion, and garlic with olive oil, then transfer to the air fryer basket. 2. Cook for about 14 minutes, flipping halfway, until charred on top. (For a toaster oven–style air fryer, the temperature remains the same; cook for 10 minutes.) 3. Remove the poblano, wrap in foil, and let it cool for 10 minutes. Remove the remaining vegetables from the basket and transfer to a food processor. 4. Spritz the tomatillos with oil and place in the air fryer basket. Cook for 10 minutes, flipping halfway, until charred. (For a toaster oven–style air fryer, the temperature and timing remain the same.) 5. Transfer to the food processor with the other vegetables. Unwrap the foil from the poblano. Peel the skin off and remove the seeds. 6. Transfer to the food processor along with the coriander, sugar (if using), and salt. Pulse the mixture until the ingredients are coarsely chopped. 7. Add 5 to 6 tablespoons water and pulse until a coarse puree forms. Transfer the salsa to a serving dish.
**Per Serving:** Calories 458; Fat 7.9g; Sodium 258mg; Carbs 8g; Fibre 64g; Sugar 14g; Protein 78g

# Crispy Cheddar Cheese Wafers

**Prep time: 4 hours 10 minutes | Cook time: 5 minutes | Serves: 48**

100g sharp Cheddar cheese, grated
55g butter
65g flour

¼ teaspoon salt
20g crisp rice cereal
Oil for misting or cooking spray

1. Cream the butter and grated cheese together. You can do it by hand, but using a stand mixer is faster and easier. 2. Combine flour and salt in a sieve. Blend it thoroughly after adding it to the cheese mixture. 3. Add cereal and mix. 4. Roll the dough into a long log with a diameter of about 2.5 cm and place it on wax paper. Wax paper should be used to wrap tightly. Chill for at least 4 hours. 5. Set the air fryer to 180°C and get ready to cook. 6. Slice the cheese roll into ½ cm thick pieces. 7. Spray air fryer basket with oil or cooking spray and place slices in a single layer, close but not touching. 8. Cook until golden brown, about 5 to 6 minutes. Place them on paper towels to cool after finished. 9. To cook the remaining cheese bites, repeat the previous step.
**Tips:** Follow steps 1 through 4 above, slice the cheese roll, and arrange the slices in a single layer on a baking sheet. The raw cheese pieces should be kept in airtight containers or bags after being placed on the cookie sheet and frozen for about an hour. The cooking time will be the same whether you cook these straight from the freezer without first thawing them (5 to 6 minutes or until golden brown).
**Per Serving:** Calories 19, Fat 1.19g; Sodium 47mg; Carbs1.49g; Fibre 0g; Sugar 0.2g; Protein 0.48g

# Cinnamon Pita Chips

**Prep time: 5 minutes | Cook time: 6 minutes | Serves: 4**

2 whole 15 cm pitas, whole grain or white
2 teaspoons cinnamon

Oil for misting or cooking spray
2 tablespoons sugar

1. Cinnamon and sugar should be combined. 2. Cut each pita in half and each half into 4 wedges. Break apart each wedge at the fold. 3. Spray oil or cooking spray on the cut side of the pita wedges. Add half of the cinnamon sugar to each of them. 4. After flipping the wedges over, drizzle oil or frying spray on the opposite side and top with the remaining cinnamon sugar. 5. Put pita wedges in the air fryer basket and fry for 2 minutes at 165°C. 6. Shake the basket, then cook for two more minutes. Reshake and heat for a further 1-2 minutes, or until crisp, as necessary. They will cook quickly at this point, so keep an eye on them.
**Tip:** The smooth side will seem darker after cooking than the rough side. Additionally, as they cool, the chips will get a little crispier.
**Per Serving:** Calories 503, Fat 4.81g; Sodium 808mg; Carbs105.15g; Fibre 14.2g; Sugar 5.43g; Protein 17.89g

# Fried Chicken Wings

**Prep time: 1 hour 20 minutes | Cook time:19 minutes | Serves: 4**

900g chicken wings
**Marinade**
½ teaspoon salt
240ml buttermilk
**Coating**
2 tablespoons poultry seasoning
125g flour
2 teaspoons salt

½ teaspoon black pepper

Oil for misting or cooking spray
110g panko breadcrumbs

1. Remove the wings' tips. Save for stock or discard. To create two pieces per wing, split the remaining wing portions at the joint. In a sizable bowl or plastic bag, put the wings. 2. Combine all the marinade ingredients, then pour it over the wings. Refrigerate for at least 1 hour but for no more than 8 hours. 3. Set the air fryer to 180°C. 4. In a plate or on wax paper, combine all the coating ingredients. 5. Shake off excess marinade from the wings before rolling them in the coating mixture. 6. Apply oil or cooking spray to both sides of each wing. 7. Arrange wings in an air fryer basket in a single layer, keeping them near together but not crammed. Cook the chicken for 17 to 19 minutes, or until the juices flow clear. 8. To cook the remaining wings, repeat step 7.
**Tip:** The second wing joint cooks more quickly than the meatier drum joint. Cook the drum joints in one batch before cooking the second batch of joints. When ready to serve, you can rewarm the first batch if necessary by placing it back in the air fryer for a minute.
**Per Serving:** Calories 456, Fat 9.4g; Sodium 1794mg; Carbs 32.8g; Fibre 1.4g; Sugar 3.56g; Protein 56.11g

# Cheese Crab Toasts

**Prep time: 10 minutes | Cook time:5 minutes | Serves: 18**

25g shredded Parmesan cheese
1 loaf artisan bread, French bread, or baguette, cut into slices ¾ cm thick
1 teaspoon Worcestershire sauce

25g shredded sharp Cheddar cheese
1 150g can flaked crabmeat, well drained
3 tablespoons light mayonnaise
½ teaspoon lemon juice

1. Mix together all ingredients except the bread slices. 2. Apply a thin layer of the crabmeat mixture to each slice of bread. (You will need approximately 12 spoonful of the crab mixture for each piece of bread measuring 5 x 3.5 cm. 3. Place in the air fryer basket in a single layer and cook for 5 minutes at 180°C, or until the toast is crispy and the tops are browned. 4. To cook the remaining crab toasts, repeat step 3.
**Note:** Crabmeat must be well drained. When combining the filling ingredients, throw away any liquid that gathers at the bottom of the dish.
**Tip:** You should freeze these as a make-ahead snack. Once prepared, freeze uncooked crab toasts on a cookie sheet by following steps 1 and 2 above. Until ready to use, store in freezer bags or airtight containers. Don't defrost. Cook frozen crab toasts as described above in an air fryer, but add an extra two minutes to the total frying time.
**Per Serving:** Calories 63, Fat 4g; Sodium 86mg; Carbs 6.07g; Fibre 1g; Sugar 3.6g; Protein 1.11g

# Kale Chips with Yogurt Sauce

**Prep Time: 10 minutes | Cook Time: 5 minutes | Serves: 4**

240g Greek yogurt
3 tablespoons lemon juice
2 tablespoons honey mustard
½ teaspoon dried oregano

1 bunch curly kale
2 tablespoons olive oil
½ teaspoon salt
⅛ teaspoon pepper

1. Combine the yogurt, lemon juice, honey mustard, and oregano in a small bowl. 2. Remove the stems and ribs from the kale, and cut the leaves into 5 – 8 cm pieces. 3. Coat the kale with olive oil, salt, and pepper. 4. Place the coated kale in the air fryer basket, and air fry them at 200°C for 5 minutes until they are crisp, tossing them halfway through. 5. Serve the kale with the yogurt sauce.
**Per Serving:** Calories 113; Fat 9.18g; Sodium 411mg; Carbs 5.72g; Fibre 1g; Sugar 3.66g; Protein 3.18g

# Crispy Apple Wedges

**Prep time: 10 minutes | Cook time:8 minutes | Serves: 4**

Oil for misting or cooking spray
½ teaspoons brown sugar
30g cornflour
30g panko breadcrumbs
30g pecans

1½ teaspoons cinnamon
1 egg white
2 teaspoons water
1 medium apple

1. Combine brown sugar, cinnamon, pecans, and panko in a food processor. Process to make small crumbs. 2. Put cornflour in a lidded basin or plastic bag. Beat the egg white and water in a small bowl until just frothy. 3. Set the air fryer to 200°C. 4. Slicing an apple into tiny wedges. The thickest edge shouldn't be any thicker than 1–1.5 cm. Peel the fruit but do not remove the core. 5. Place apple wedges in a basin or bag of cornflour, close it, and shake to coat. 6. Roll wedges in the crumbs after dipping them in egg wash and shaking off the excess. Spray some oil on. 7. Arrange the apples in a single layer and cook them in the air fryer basket for 5 minutes. Shake the basket and separate any clumped-together apples. 8. Lightly mist with oil and cook for a further 3 to 4 minutes, or until crispy.
**Per Serving:** Calories 117, Fat 4.7g; Sodium 26mg; Carbs 18.09g; Fibre 2.3g; Sugar 6.85g; Protein 1.87g

# Curried Sweet Potato Fries

**Prep Time: 5 minutes | Cook Time: 12 minutes | Serves: 4**

120g sour cream
135g mango chutney
3 teaspoons curry powder, divided
230g frozen sweet potato fries

1 tablespoon olive oil
Pinch salt
Freshly ground black pepper

1. Mix the sour cream, chutney, and 1½ teaspoons of curry powder in a small bowl. Set aside for later. 2. Place the sweet potatoes in a medium bowl, drizzle them with the olive oil, and sprinkle them with the remaining 1½ teaspoons curry powder, salt, and pepper, then transfer them to the air fryer basket. 3. Bake the potatoes at 200°C for 8 to 12 minutes until they are crisp and golden brown, tossing them halfway through. 4. Enjoy the sweet potatoes with the chutney dip.
**Per Serving:** Calories 255; Fat 7.03g; Sodium 74mg; Carbs 45.09g; Fibre 4.1g; Sugar 2.92g; Protein 4.4g

# Cumin Aubergine Fries

**Prep time: 10 minutes | Cook time:8 minutes | Serves: 4**

Oil for misting or cooking spray
1 teaspoon cumin
1 teaspoon garlic powder
½ teaspoon salt
1 medium aubergine

1 teaspoon ground coriander
2 tablespoons water
110g crushed panko breadcrumbs
1 large egg

1. Peel the aubergine and slice it into 1.5 to 2.5 cm-thick fat fry. 2. Turn the air fryer on at 200°C. 3. Combine the coriander, cumin, garlic, and salt in a small cup. 4. In a shallow plate, mix 1 teaspoon of the spice mix with the panko crumbs. 5. Add the remaining seasoning to the bowl with the aubergine fries and toss to incorporate. 6. Combine eggs and water and pour over french fries made from aubergine. Stir to coat. 7. Shake off excess egg wash from the aubergine before rolling it in panko crumbs. 8. Spray with oil. 9. Fill the air fryer basket with half the fries. It's okay if they slightly overlap, but you should only have one layer. 10. Cook for five minutes. Shake the basket, lightly spritz with oil, and cook for an additional 2 to 3 minutes, or until crispy and golden. 11. To cook the remaining aubergine, repeat step 10.
**Per Serving:** Calories 72, Fat 1.73g; Sodium 410mg; Carbs 13.43g; Fibre 5.4g; Sugar 7.55g; Protein 3.23g

# Artichoke Triangles

**Prep Time: 15 minutes | Cook Time: 9 minutes | Serves: 6**

1 egg white
55g minced drained artichoke hearts
3 tablespoons grated mozzarella cheese

½ teaspoon dried thyme
6 sheets frozen puff pastry , thawed
2 tablespoons melted butter

1. Combine the ricotta cheese, egg white, artichoke hearts, mozzarella cheese, and thyme in a small bowl. 2. Cover the pastry with a damp kitchen towel before using to avoid they dry out. 3. Place one sheet on the work surface at a time, and cut one into thirds lengthwise. 4. Put about 1½ teaspoons of the filling on each strip at the base, fold the bottom right-hand tip of puff pastry over the filling to meet the other side in a triangle, then continue folding in a triangle. 5. Brush each triangle with butter to seal the edges. Do the same with the remaining pastry and filling. 6. Bake the triangles at 205°C for 3 to 4 minutes until they are golden brown, you can bake them in 3 batches. 7. Serve warm.
**Per Serving:** Calories 121; Fat 6.64g; Sodium 231mg; Carbs 11.82g; Fibre 1.2g; Sugar 0.73g; Protein 3.51g

# Homemade Arancini

**Prep Time: 15 minutes | Cook Time: 22 minutes | Serves: 6**

400g cooked and cooled rice or leftover risotto
2 eggs, beaten
150g panko bread crumbs, divided
50g grated Parmesan cheese

2 tablespoons minced fresh basil
16 1.5-cm cubes mozzarella cheese
2 tablespoons olive oil

1. Combine the rice, eggs, 50g of the bread crumbs, Parmesan cheese, and basil in a medium bowl, and then make them into sixteen 3.5-cm balls. 2. Make a hole in each balls, and insert a mozzarella cube. Form the rice mixture firmly around the cheese. 3. Mix the remaining bread crumbs with olive oil in another bowl, and then coat the rice balls with them. 4. Air Fry the rice balls at 205°C for 8 to 11 minutes until golden brown, you can cook them in batches. 5. Serve warm.
**Per Serving:** Calories 331; Fat 17.85g; Sodium 391mg; Carbs 40.36g; Fibre 9.5g; Sugar 2.13g; Protein 13.94g

# Pesto Bruschetta

**Prep Time: 10 minutes | Cook Time: 8 minutes | Serves: 4**

8 slices French bread, 1 cm thick
2 tablespoons softened butter
120g shredded mozzarella cheese

115g basil pesto
155g chopped grape tomatoes
2 green onions, thinly sliced

1. Spread the butter on the bread slices, place the bread slices in the air fryer basket with butter-side up, and then bake them at 175°C for 3 to 5 minutes until they are light golden brown. 2. When the time is up, top each bread slice with some cheese, and then resume baking them for 1 to 3 minutes until the cheese melts. 3. Mix the tomatoes, green onions, and pesto in a small bowl. 4. After baking, transfer the bread slices to the serving plate, and top them with the pesto mixture. Enjoy.
**Per Serving:** Calories 304; Fat 7.11g; Sodium 675mg; Carbs 44.17g; Fibre 2.8g; Sugar 8.59g; Protein 16.98g

# Fried Tortellini with Mayonnaise

### Prep Time: 10 minutes | Cook Time: 20 minutes | Serves: 4

180g mayonnaise
2 tablespoons mustard
1 egg
65g flour

½ teaspoon dried oregano
150g bread crumbs
2 tablespoons olive oil
300g frozen cheese tortellini

1. Combine the mayonnaise and mustard in a small bowl. Set aside. 2. Beat the egg in another bowl, and mix the flour and oregano in the third bowl, and then combine the bread crumbs with olive oil in the fourth bowl. 3. Dip the tortellini into the egg, then into the flour and into the egg again, and coat them with the bread crumbs. 4. Air Fry them at 195°C for 10 minutes until they are crisp and golden brown on the outside, shaking the basket halfway through. 5. Serve the tortellini with the mayonnaise.
**Per Serving:** Calories 500; Fat 28.22g; Sodium 743mg; Carbs 45.96g; Fibre 2.7g; Sugar 1.92g; Protein 15.29g

# Breaded Prawn Toast

### Prep Time: 15 minutes | Cook Time: 12 minutes | Serves: 6

3 slices firm white bread
95g finely chopped peeled and deveined raw prawn
1 egg white
2 cloves garlic, minced
2 tablespoons corn flour

¼ teaspoon ground ginger
Pinch salt
Freshly ground black pepper
2 tablespoons olive oil

1. Cut the crusts from the bread, and crumble the crusts to make bread crumbs. Set aside. 2. Mix the prawn with the egg white, garlic, corn flour, ginger, salt, and pepper in a bowl. 3. Spread the prawn mixture evenly on the bread to the edges, and then cut each slice into 4 strips. 4. Mix the bread crumbs with olive oil, and coat the prawn with them. 5. Place the prawn mixture in the air fryer basket in a single layer, and Air Fry them at 175°C for 3 to 6 minutes until crisp and golden brown. 6. Serve hot.
**Per Serving:** Calories 102; Fat 5.02g; Sodium 227mg; Carbs 9.02g; Fibre 1.3g; Sugar 0.75g; Protein 5.09g

# Ranch Chicken French Bread Pizza

### Prep time: 10 minutes | Cook time: 12 minutes | Serves: 8

Oil, for spraying
1 loaf French bread, cut in half and split lengthwise
4 tablespoons unsalted butter, melted
280g shredded or diced rotisserie chicken
100g cream cheese

3 tablespoons buffalo sauce, and more for serving
2 tablespoons dry ranch seasoning
240g shredded mozzarella cheese
80g crumbled blue cheese

1. Prepare the air fryer basket by lining it with parchment and spray lightly with oil. 2. Brush the cut sides of the bread with the melted butter. Place the bread in the prepared basket. You may need to work in batches, depending on the size of your air fryer. 3. Cook at 205°C for 5 to 7 minutes, or until the bread is toasted. 4. Mix the chicken, cream cheese, buffalo sauce, and ranch seasoning in a medium bowl. 5. Divide the mixture equally among the toasted bread and spread in an even layer. 6. Top with the mozzarella cheese and blue cheese and cook for another 3 to 5 minutes, or until the cheese is melted. 7. Set aside and cool for 2 to 3 minutes before cutting into 5 cm slices. Serve with additional buffalo sauce for drizzling.
**Per Serving:** Calories 1093; Fat 57g; Sodium 1509mg; Carbs 74.8g; Fibre 3.5g; Sugar 7.5g; Protein 67g

# Savory Tater Tot Kebabs

**Prep time: 15 minutes | Cook time: 20 minutes | Serves: 6**

Oil, for spraying
1 (500g) bag frozen tater tots
50g shredded cheddar cheese

55g bacon bits
½ teaspoon granulated garlic
2 tablespoons chopped fresh chives, for garnish

1. Preheat the air fryer to 205°C. Prepare the air fryer basket lining it with parchment and spray lightly with oil. 2. Place the tater tots in the prepared basket. They should cover the bottom with a few extra on top. Work in batches as needed. 3. Cook for 15 minutes, shaking after 7 or 8 minutes. 4. Let cool to room temperature. Thread 5 or 6 tots on each skewer. 5. Place the skewers in the air fryer, sprinkle with the cheese, bacon bits, and garlic, and cook until just golden brown and crispy, for another 5 minutes. 6. Sprinkle with the chives and serve.
**Per Serving:** Calories 175; Fat 8.2g; Sodium 272mg; Carbs 18.6g; Fibre 1g; Sugar 14.5g; Protein 7.5g

# Waffle Fry Nachos with Bacon

**Prep time: 5 minutes | Cook time: 11 minutes | Serves: 4**

Oil, for spraying
1 (500g) package frozen waffle fries
100g shredded cheddar cheese
2 tablespoons bacon bits

1 tablespoon canned diced green chilies
1 tablespoon sliced olives
70g salsa of choice
1 tablespoon sour cream

1. Prepare the air fryer basket by lining it with parchment and spray lightly with oil. Place the waffle fries in the prepared basket and spray lightly with oil. 2. Cook at 190°C for 8 minutes. Transfer to an air fryer–safe baking pan. 3. Top with the cheese, bacon bits, green chilies, and olives. Raise the heat to 220°C and cook for 2 to 3 minutes, or until the cheese is melted. 4. Top with the salsa and sour cream before serving.
**Per Serving:** Calories 511; Fat 32g; Sodium 1072mg; Carbs 45.6g; Fibre 7.1g; Sugar 0.7g; Protein 12.3g

# Wrapped Sausages

**Prep time: 15 minutes | Cook time: 12 minutes | Serves: 7**

Oil, for spraying
1 (300g) package thick-cut bacon
1 (300g) package cocktail sausages

2 teaspoons chili powder
2 tablespoons maple syrup
2 tablespoons packed light brown sugar

1. Prepare the air fryer basket by lining it with parchment and spray lightly with oil. (The parchment will catch drippings. If your air fryer has an outer tray, you can also line it with foil.) 2. Cut each bacon strip lengthwise into thirds and wrap a piece around each sausage, securing with a toothpick. 3. Place the wrapped sausages in the prepared basket in a single layer and sprinkle with the chili powder. Work in batches as needed. Brush the sausages with the maple syrup and sprinkle with the brown sugar. 4. Cook at 170°C for 6 minutes, flip, and cook for another 6 minutes, or until the bacon is crisp. 5. Remove the toothpicks and serve immediately.
**Per Serving:** Calories 476; Fat 18g; Sodium 924mg; Carbs 72.6g; Fibre 2.4g; Sugar 64.5g; Protein 12.5g

# Thai-style Cauliflower Bites

**Prep time: 15 minutes | Cook time: 15 minutes | Serves: 6**

Oil, for spraying
1 medium head cauliflower, cut into florets
2 tablespoons olive oil
2 teaspoons granulated garlic

¼ teaspoon smoked paprika
120ml–180ml sweet chili sauce
¼ teaspoon sesame seeds

1. Preheat the air fryer to 205°C. Prepare the air fryer basket by lining it with parchment and spraying lightly with oil. 2. Add the cauliflower in a large bowl and drizzle with olive oil, tossing until fully coated. Sprinkle with the garlic and paprika and toss again until coated. 3. Place the cauliflower in the prepared basket, taking care not to overlap the pieces. Work in batches as needed. 4. Cook for 15 minutes, or until the cauliflowers are browned and crispy, flipping every 5 minutes. 5. Transfer the cauliflowers to a large serving bowl and toss with the sweet chili sauce and sesame seeds before serving.
**Per Serving:** Calories 77; Fat 4.8g; Sodium 318mg; Carbs 7g; Fibre 2.3g; Sugar 3.3g; Protein 1.5g

# Fried Crusted Cheese Ravioli

**Prep time: 10 minutes | Cook time: 5 minutes | Serves: 8**

Oil, for spraying
2 large eggs
105g panko bread crumbs
25g grated Parmesan cheese
1 teaspoon onion powder

1 teaspoon granulated garlic
½ teaspoon dry Italian dressing mix
½ teaspoon salt
1 (500g) package refrigerated cheese ravioli

1. Preheat the air fryer to 205°C. Prepare the air fryer basket by lining it with parchment and spray lightly with oil. 2. Whisk the eggs in a suitable bowl and set aside. 3. In another medium bowl, mix together the bread crumbs, Parmesan cheese, onion powder, garlic, Italian dressing mix, and salt. 4. Add the ravioli to the eggs and toss gently to coat. 5. Transfer the ravioli to the bread crumb mixture and toss until evenly coated. 6. Arrange the coated ravioli in a single layer in the prepared basket. You may need to work in batches, depending on the size of your air fryer. Spray lightly with oil. 7. Cook the ravioli in your air fryer for 3 to 5 minutes, or until hot and crispy.
**Per Serving:** Calories 103; Fat 3.4g; Sodium 476mg; Carbs 13.4g; Fibre 1.2g; Sugar 3.2g; Protein 4.8g

# Worcestershire Cheese Bread Bowl

**Prep time: 10 minutes | Cook time: 28 minutes | Serves: 6**

1 (15 cm) round loaf bread, unsliced
2 tablespoons olive oil
150g cream cheese, at room temperature
120g mayonnaise
60ml whole milk

100g shredded cheese
100g shredded provolone cheese
25g grated Parmesan cheese
2 spring onions , sliced
1 teaspoon Worcestershire sauce

1. Cut off the top 2.5 cm of the bread. Use a serrated bread knife to cut around the inside of the loaf, leaving about a 2.5 cm shell. Do not cut through the bottom. Cut the pieces of bread and the top of the loaf into 2.5 cm cubes and drizzle with the olive oil. 2. Heat the air fryer to 190°C before cooking. Put the bread cubes in the air fryer basket and bake for 5 to 8 minutes, shaking halfway through cooking time, until toasted. Place in a serving bowl. Keep the air fryer set to 190°C. 3. Meanwhile, beat the cream cheese with the mayonnaise and milk until smooth. Stir in the shredded cheese, provolone, and Parmesan cheeses, spring onions , and Worcestershire sauce. 4. Divide the cheese mixture into the centre of the bread shell. Put the filled bread in the air fryer basket and place the basket in the air fryer. 5. Bake the cheese bread at 190°C for 15 to 20 minutes until the cheese is melted and starts to brown on top, stirring the mixture halfway through cooking time. Serve with the toasted bread and bread sticks, if desired.
**Per Serving:** Calories 364; Fat 32g; Sodium 674mg; Carbs 4.6g; Fibre 0.4g; Sugar 3g; Protein 15g

# Apricots and Cheese in Blankets

**Prep time: 20 minutes | Cook time: 24 minutes | Serves: 6**

6 dried apricots, halved lengthwise
4 tablespoons (50g) cream cheese
½ sheet frozen puff pastry, thawed

4 tablespoons honey mustard
2 tablespoons butter, melted

1. Stuff each apricot half with a teaspoon of cream cheese and set aside. 2. Roll out the puff pastry until it is 15 by 30 cm. Cut in half lengthwise for two 8-by-30-cm rectangles. Cut each rectangle into six 8 cm strips for a total of 12 puff pastry strips. 3. Spread 1 teaspoon of honey mustard onto each strip. Place a filled apricot on each strip and roll up the pastry, pinching the seam closed but leaving the ends open. 4. Place 6 filled pastries in the air fryer basket. Then brush the top of each with some of the melted butter. 5. Set or preheat the air fryer to 190°C. Put the basket in the air fryer. Bake the pastries for 8 to 12 minutes or until the pastry is golden brown. 6. Repeat with the other six pastries, then serve.
**Per Serving:** Calories 190; Fat 16.5g; Sodium 320mg; Carbs 8g; Fibre 1g; Sugar 5.2g; Protein 3.6g

# Sesame Mushroom Toast

**Prep time: 20 minutes | Cook time: 8 minutes per batch | Serves: 6**

2 teaspoons olive oil
2 (100g) cans sliced mushrooms, drained
3 spring onions, sliced
1 tablespoon grated fresh ginger

1 tablespoon soy sauce
3 slices whole-wheat bread
2 tablespoons sesame seeds

1. Heat the olive oil in a medium saucepan over medium heat. Add the mushrooms and cook, stirring often, for 3 to 4 minutes or until the mushrooms are dry. 2. Add the spring onions, ginger, and soy sauce and cook for another 3 minutes or until the mushrooms have absorbed the soy sauce. 3. Transfer the mixture to a blender or food processor and process until it forms a paste. 4. Cut the bread slices into fourths, making triangles. Spread the mushroom mixture onto the bread triangles, dividing evenly, then sprinkle with the sesame seeds. 5. Heat the air fryer to 190°C before cooking. Working in batches, place the triangles in the air fryer basket in a single layer. Fry for 7 to 8 minutes or until the toast is crisp. Repeat with the remaining triangles. Serve.
**Per Serving:** Calories 90; Fat 4.3g; Sodium 117mg; Carbs 9.8g; Fibre 2g; Sugar 2.2g; Protein 4g

# Focaccia Bites with Grapes

**Prep time: 15 minutes | Cook time: 28 minutes | Serves: 4**

125g plain flour
½ teaspoon sea salt
1½ teaspoons baking powder
80ml whole milk

4 tablespoons olive oil, divided
100g halved red grapes
2 teaspoons fresh thyme

1. In a medium bowl, combine the flour, salt, and baking powder and mix well. 2. Add the milk and 3 tablespoons of the olive oil and stir just until a dough forms. Divide the dough into two balls. 3. Cut two pieces of parchment paper to fit in your air fryer basket. Press the dough onto each piece of paper, spreading the dough so it almost fills the paper. 4. Dimple the dough with your fingers. Drizzle both with the remaining 1 tablespoon olive oil. 5. Put the grapes on the dough, cut-side down, and press down gently. Sprinkle with the thyme. Place one of the parchment pieces with dough in the air fryer basket. 6. Set or preheat the air fryer to 175°C. Put the basket in the air fryer and bake for 11 to 14 minutes or until the bread is golden brown. Remove the focaccia and repeat with the remaining dough. 7. Cut into squares and serve.
**Per Serving:** Calories 271; Fat 14.5g; Sodium 303mg; Carbs 32g; Fibre 1.2g; Sugar 6.6g; Protein 4g

# Chapter 7 Dessert Recipes

# Gorgeous Marble Cheesecake

**Prep Time: 10 minutes | Cook Time: 20 minutes | Serves: 8**

60 g digestive biscuit crumbs
3 tablespoons butter, at room temperature
1½ (200 g) packages cream cheese, at room temperature
55 g sugar

2 eggs, beaten
1 tablespoon plain flour
1 teaspoon vanilla extract
75 g chocolate syrup

1. Stir the biscuit crumbs and butter in a bowl. Press the crust into the bottom of a 15-by-5-cm round baking pan and freeze to set while you prepare the filling. 2. Stir together the cream cheese and sugar in a bowl until mixed well. 3. One at a time, beat in the eggs. Add the flour and vanilla and stir to combine. 4. Transfer ⅔ cup of filling to a small bowl and stir in the chocolate syrup until combined. 5. Insert the crisper plate into the air fryer basket, and preheat the air fryer at 160°C for 3 minutes on Bake mode. 6. Pour the vanilla filling into the pan with the crust. Drop the chocolate filling over the vanilla filling by the spoonful. With a clean butter knife stir the fillings in a zigzag pattern to marbleize them. Do not let the knife touch the crust. 7. Once the unit is preheated, place the pan into the air fryer basket. 8. Bake the food at 160°C for 20 minutes. 9. When the cooking is done, the cheesecake should be just set. Cool the dish on a wire rack for 1 hour. Refrigerate the cheesecake until firm before slicing.
**Per Serving:** Calories 214; Fat 15.62g; Sodium 206mg; Carbs 13.79g; Fibre 0.3g; Sugar 10.44g; Protein 4.84mg

# Ultimate Chocolate Bread Pudding

**Prep Time: 10 minutes | Cook Time: 10 minutes | Serves: 4**

Nonstick baking spray
1 egg
1 egg yolk
180 ml chocolate milk
2 tablespoons cocoa powder

3 tablespoons light brown sugar
3 tablespoons peanut butter
1 teaspoon vanilla extract
5 slices firm white bread, cubed

1. Spray a 15-by-5-cm round baking pan with the baking spray. 2. In a medium bowl, whisk the egg, egg yolk, chocolate milk, cocoa powder, brown sugar, peanut butter, and vanilla until thoroughly combined. Stir in the bread cubes and let soak for 10 minutes. Spoon this mixture into the prepared pan. 3. Place the pan into the air fryer basket, and bake the food at 160°C for 12 minutes. 4. Check the pudding after about 10 minutes. It is done when it is firm to the touch. If not, resume cooking. 5. When the cooking is complete, let the pudding cool for 5 minutes. 6. Serve warm.
**Per Serving:** Calories 277; Fat 7.45g; Sodium 239 mg; Carbs 43.73g; Fibre 4.7g; Sugar 10.83g; Protein 11.02g

# Sweet Pineapple Cheese Wontons

**Prep Time: 15 minutes | Cook Time: 15 minutes | Serves: 5**

1 (200 g) package cream cheese
165 g finely chopped fresh pineapple

20 wonton wrappers
Cooking oil spray

1. Add the cream cheese to a small microwave-safe bowl, and heat the cream cheese in the microwave on high power for 20 seconds to soften. 2. Stir the cream cheese and pineapple until mixed well in a bowl. 3. Lay out the wonton wrappers on a work surface. 4. Spoon 1½ teaspoons of the cream cheese mixture onto each wrapper, do not to overfill. 5. Fold each wrapper diagonally across to form a triangle. Bring the 2 bottom corners up toward each other. Do not close the wrapper yet. Bring up the 2 open sides and push out any air. Squeeze the open edges together to seal. 6. Insert the crisper plate into the air fryer basket and the air fryer basket into the unit, and then preheat the air fryer at 200°C for 3 minutes. 7. Once the unit is preheated, spray the crisper plate with cooking oil. 8. Place the wontons into the air fryer basket, and spray the wontons with the cooking oil. 9. Air Fry the wontons at 200°C for 18 minutes. 10. After 10 minutes, remove the air fryer basket, flip each wonton, and spray them with more oil. Reinsert the air fryer basket to resume cooking for 5 to 8 minutes more until the wontons are light golden brown and crisp. 11. If cooking in batches, remove the cooked wontons from the air fryer basket and repeat steps 7, 8, and 9 for the remaining wontons. 12. When the cooking is complete, let the wontons cool for 5 minutes before serving.
**Per Serving:** Calories 552; Fat 16.59g; Sodium 942mg; Carbs 83.61g; Fibre 2.7g; Sugar 8.88g; Protein 16.16g

# Irresistible Honey-Roasted Pears

**Prep Time: 7 minutes | Cook Time: 25 minutes | Serves: 4**

2 large pears, halved lengthwise and seeded
3 tablespoons honey
1 tablespoon unsalted butter

½ teaspoon ground cinnamon
30 g walnuts, chopped
60 g part-skim ricotta cheese, divided

1. Insert the crisper plate into the air fryer basket, and preheat the air fryer at 175°C for 3 minutes on Air Roast mode. 2. In a 15-by-5-cm round pan, place the pears cut-side up. 3. In a small microwave-safe bowl, melt the honey, butter, and cinnamon. Brush this mixture over the cut sides of the pears. Pour 3 tablespoons of water around the pears in the pan. 4. Once the unit is preheated, place the pan into the air fryer basket. 5. Air Roast the food at 175°C for 23 minutes. 6. After about 18 minutes, check the pears. They should be tender when pierced with a fork and slightly crisp on the edges. If not, resume cooking. 7. When the cooking is complete, baste the pears once with the liquid in the pan. Carefully remove the pears from the pan and place on a serving plate. Drizzle each with some liquid from the pan, sprinkle the walnuts on top, and serve with a spoonful of ricotta cheese.

**Per Serving:** Calories 194; Fat 6.52g; Sodium 18mg; Carbs 32.35g; Fibre 3.9g; Sugar 24.32g; Protein 3.1g

# Unbeatable Gooey Lemon Bars

**Prep Time: 15 minutes | Cook Time: 25 minutes | Serves: 6**

95 g whole-wheat pastry flour
2 tablespoons icing sugar
55 g butter, melted
95 g granulated sugar
1 tablespoon packed grated lemon zest
60 ml freshly squeezed lemon juice

⅛ teaspoon sea salt
60 g unsweetened plain applesauce
2 teaspoons cornflour
¾ teaspoon baking powder
Cooking oil spray (sunflower, safflower, or refined coconut)

1. Stir the flour, icing sugar, and melted butter just until well combined in a bowl. Place in the refrigerator. 2. Stir the granulated sugar, lemon zest and juice, salt, applesauce, cornflour, and baking powder in a bowl. 3. Insert the crisper plate into the air fryer basket, and preheat the air fryer at 175°C for 3 minutes on Bake mode. 4. Spray a 15-by-5-cm round pan lightly with cooking oil. Remove the crust mixture from the refrigerator and gently press it into the bottom of the prepared pan in an even layer. 5. Once the unit is preheated, place the pan into the air fryer basket. 6. Bake the dish at 175°C for 25 minutes. 7. After 5 minutes, check the crust. It should be slightly firm to the touch. Remove the pan and spread the lemon filling over the crust. Reinsert the pan into the air fryer basket and resume baking for 18 to 20 minutes. 8. When baking is complete, let cool for 30 minutes. Refrigerate to cool completely. Cut into pieces.

**Per Serving:** Calories 173; Fat 8.14g; Sodium 114 mg; Carbs 24.91g; Fibre 1.8; Sugar 12.1g; Protein 2.13 g

# Delicious Baked Apples

**Prep Time: 6 minutes | Cook Time: 20 minutes | Serves: 4**

4 small Granny Smith apples
40 g chopped walnuts
55 g light brown sugar
2 tablespoons butter, melted

1 teaspoon ground cinnamon
½ teaspoon ground nutmeg
120 g water, or apple juice

1. Cut off the top third of the apples. Spoon out the core and some of the flesh and discard. Place the apples in a small air fryer baking pan. 2. Insert the crisper plate into the air fryer basket and the air fryer basket into the unit. Preheat the unit by selecting BAKE, setting the temperature to 175°C, and setting the time to 3 minutes. Select START/STOP to begin. 3. Stir together the walnuts, brown sugar, melted butter, cinnamon, and nutmeg in a bowl. Spoon this mixture into the centres of the hollowed-out apples. 4. Once the unit is preheated, pour the water into the crisper plate. Place the baking pan into the air fryer basket. 5. Select BAKE, set the temperature to 175°C, and set the time to 20 minutes. Select START/STOP to begin. 6. When the cooking is complete, the apples should be bubbly and fork-tender.

**Per Serving:** Calories 188; Fat 10.76g; Sodium 52mg; Carbs 22.08g; Fibre 4.9g; Sugar 14.28g; Protein 1.91g

# Delicious Macaroon Bites

**Prep time: 15 minutes | Cook time: 15 minutes | Serves: 2**

4 egg whites
½ teaspoon vanilla
½ teaspoon EZ-Sweet

4½ teaspoon water
100 g unsweetened coconut

1. Preheat your fryer to 190°C. Combine the egg whites, vanilla, EZ-Sweet, water and coconut. 2. Put into the fryer and reduce the heat to 160°C. Cook for 15 minutes. Serve!
**Per Serving:** Calories 254; Fat 7.9g; Sodium 2544mg; Carbs 2g; Fibre 10g; Sugar 6g; Protein 11g

# Creamy Choco-berry Fudge Sauce

**Prep time: 5 minutes | Cook time: 5 minutes | Serves: 2**

100 g cream cheese, softened
80 g 90% chocolate Lindt bar, chopped
50 g powdered erythritol

60 g heavy cream
1 tablespoon Monin sugar-free raspberry syrup

1. In a large frying pan, melt the cream cheese and chocolate. 2. Stir in the sweetener. Remove from the heat and allow to cool. 3. Once cool, mix in the cream and syrup. Serve!
**Per Serving:** Calories 321; Fat 7.9g; Sodium 789mg; Carbs 741g; Fibre 87g; Sugar 29g; Protein 93g

# Frosted Chocolate Cake

**Prep time: 10 minutes | Cook time: 25 minutes | Serves: 6**

**For the Cake**
90g (whole-wheat pastry, gluten-free plain, or plain)
100g organic sugar
2 tablespoons cocoa powder
**For the Frosting**
3 tablespoons vegan margarine
155g icing sugar
120ml nondairy milk
2½ tablespoons neutral flavoured oil (sunflower, safflower, or melted refined coconut)
½ tablespoon apple cider vinegar

½ teaspoon baking soda
⅛ teaspoon sea salt

½ teaspoon vanilla
Coconut oil (for greasing)
5 tablespoons cocoa powder
2 teaspoons vanilla
⅛ teaspoon sea salt

**To make the cake:** 1. Stir together the sugar, flour, cocoa powder, baking soda, and salt in a medium bowl with a wire whisk. When thoroughly combined, add the milk, oil, vinegar, and vanilla. Stir just until well combined. 2. Preheat the air fryer to 175°C for 2 minutes. 3. Grease a 15 cm round, 5 cm-deep baking pan liberally with some coconut oil to avoid the cake from sticking to the pan. Add the batter to the oiled pan and bake for 25 minutes, or until a knife inserted in the centre comes out clean.
**To make the frosting:** 1. Cream together the vegan margarine and icing sugar in a medium bowl with an electric beater. 2. Add the cocoa powder, vanilla, and salt and whip with the beaters until thoroughly combined and fluffy. With a rubber spatula, occasionally scrape down the sides as needed. Refrigerate until ready to use.
**To assemble:** 1. Cool the cake completely, and then run a knife around the edges of the baking pan. Turn it upside-down on a plate so it can be frosted on the sides and top. 2. Allow the cake to cool until no longer hot, usually about 10 minutes. When the frosting is no longer cold, use a butter knife or small spatula to frost the sides and top. Cut into slices and enjoy.
**Per Serving:** Calories 296; Fat 13g; Sodium 222mg; Carbs 45g; Fibre 3.5g; Sugar 30g; Protein 3.8g

# Strawberry Yogurt

**Prep time: 30 minutes | Cook time: 0 minutes | Serves: 4**

155 g sugar-free strawberry preserves
15 g Splenda

480 g Fage Total 0% Greek Yogurt
Ice cream maker

1. In a food processor, purée the strawberries. 2. Add the strawberry preserves and sugar. Add the Greek yogurt and fully mix. 3. Put into the ice cream maker for 25-30 minute. Serve!
**Per Serving:** Calories 458; Fat 7.9g; Sodium 258mg; Carbs 8g; Fibre 64g; Sugar 14g; Protein 78g

# Cream Berries Layer Cake

**Prep time: 10 minutes | Cook time: 5 minutes | Serves: 1**

¼ lemon pound cake
60 g whipping cream
½ teaspoon Sweetener

⅛ teaspoon orange flavour
145 g mixed berries

1. Using a sharp knife, divide the lemon cake into small cubes. Dice the strawberries. 2. Combine the whipping cream, Sweetener, and orange flavour. Layer the fruit, cake and cream in a glass. Serve!
**Per Serving:** Calories 789; Fat 7.9g; Sodium 412mg; Carbs 2g; Fibre 69g; Sugar 47g; Protein 12g

# Chocolate Coconut Pudding

**Prep time: 60 minutes | Cook time: 0 minutes | Serves: 2**

240 ml coconut milk
2 tablespoons cacao powder or organic cocoa
½ teaspoon Sugar powder extract or 2 tablespoon honey/

maple syrup
½ tablespoon quality gelatin
1 tablespoon water

1. On a medium heat, combine the coconut milk, cocoa and sweetener. 2. In a separate bowl, mix in the gelatin and water. Add to the pan and stir until fully dissolved. 3. Pour into small dishes and refrigerate for 1 hour. Serve!
**Per Serving:** Calories222; Fat 7g; Sodium 634mg; Carbs 9g; Fibre 85g; Sugar 78g; Protein 32g

# Maple Chocolate Chip Cookies

**Prep time: 10 minutes | Cook time: 7 minutes | Serves: 6**

1 tablespoon refined coconut oil, melted
1 tablespoon maple syrup
1 tablespoon nondairy milk
½ teaspoon vanilla
30g plus 2 tablespoons whole-wheat pastry flour or plain gluten-free flour

2 tablespoons coconut sugar
¼ teaspoon sea salt
¼ teaspoon baking powder
2 tablespoons vegan chocolate chips
Cooking oil spray (sunflower, safflower, or refined coconut)

1. Stir together the oil, maple syrup, milk, and vanilla in a medium bowl. Add the flour, coconut sugar, salt, and baking powder. Stir just until thoroughly combined. Stir in the chocolate chips. 2. Preheat the air fryer basket (with a 15 cm round, 5 cm-deep baking pan inside) for 2 minutes. Then, spray the pan lightly with oil. Add the batter by teaspoonful to the pan, leaving a little room in between in case they spread out a bit. Bake at 175°C for 7 minutes, or until lightly browned. Be careful not to overcook. 3. Gently transfer to a cooling rack (or plate). Repeat as desired, making all of the cookies at once, or keeping the batter on hand in the fridge to be used later (it will keep refrigerated in an airtight container for about a week). Enjoy warm if possible!
**Per Serving:** Calories 89; Fat 3g; Sodium 116mg; Carbs 14g; Fibre 0g; Sugar 6g; Protein 1g

# Cranberry Cream

**Prep time: 20 minutes | Cook time: 0 minutes | Serves: 1**

130 g mashed cranberries
10 g Sweetener
2 teaspoons natural cherry flavouring

2 teaspoons natural rum flavouring
240 g organic heavy cream

1. Combine the mashed cranberries, sweetener, cherry flavouring and rum flavourings. Cover and refrigerate for 20 minutes. 2. Whip the heavy cream until soft peaks form. Layer the whipped cream and cranberry mixture. 3. Top with fresh cranberries, mint leaves or grated dark chocolate. Serve!
**Per Serving:** Calories 321; Fat 7.9g; Sodium 789mg; Carbs 741g; Fibre 87g; Sugar 29g; Protein 93g

# Courgette Bread

**Prep time: 10 minutes | Cook time: 40 minutes | Serves: 12**

200g coconut flour
2 teaspoons baking powder
150g Erythritol
120ml coconut oil, melted
1 teaspoon apple cider vinegar

1 teaspoon vanilla extract
3 eggs, beaten
1 courgette, grated
1 teaspoon ground cinnamon

1. Combine baking powder, erythritol, coconut oil, apple cider vinegar, vanilla extract, eggs, courgette, and ground cinnamon in a bowl with the coconut flour. 2. Spread the ingredients out into the shape of bread in the air fryer basket. 3. Bake the bread for 40 minutes at 175°C.
**Per Serving:** Calories 121, Fat 11.58g; Sodium 68mg; Carbs 2.42g; Fibre 0.6g; Sugar 1.3g; Protein 2.56g

# Poppy Seed Muffins

**Prep time: 10 minutes | Cook time: 10 minutes | Serves: 5**

1 teaspoon baking powder
2 tablespoons Erythritol
125g coconut flour
5 tablespoons coconut oil, softened

1 egg, beaten
1 teaspoon vanilla extract
1 tablespoon poppy seeds

1. In the mixing bowl, mix coconut oil with egg, vanilla extract, poppy seeds, baking powder, Erythritol, and coconut flour. 2. When the mixture is homogenous, pour it into the muffin molds and transfer it to the air fryer basket. 3. Cook the muffins for 10 minutes at 185°C.
**Per Serving:** Calories 165, Fat 16.36g; Sodium 72mg; Carbs 3.05g; Fibre 0.9g; Sugar 1.54g; Protein 2.46g

# Lime Almond Pie

**Prep time: 10 minutes | Cook time: 35 minutes | Serves: 8**

2 tablespoons coconut oil, melted
1 teaspoon lime zest, grated
1 teaspoon baking powder
2 eggs, beaten
150g Erythritol

25g. almonds, chopped
25g almond flour
1 teaspoon vanilla extract
½ teaspoon apple cider vinegar

1. Mix all ingredients in the mixing bowl and whisk until smooth. 2. Then pour the mixture into the baking pan and flatten gently. 3. Put the baking pan in the air fryer and cook the pie at 185°C for 35 minutes.
**Per Serving:** Calories 85, Fat 7.6g; Sodium 26mg; Carbs 1.48g; Fibre 0.5g; Sugar 0.43g; Protein 3g

# Flavoured Vanilla Scones

**Prep time: 20 minutes | Cook time: 10 minutes | Serves: 6**

60g heavy cream
1 teaspoon vanilla extract
100g coconut flour
½ teaspoon baking powder

1 teaspoon apple cider vinegar
2 teaspoons mascarpone
1 tablespoon Erythritol
Cooking spray

1. Coconut flour, baking powder, apple cider vinegar, mascarpone, heavy cream, vanilla extract, and erythritol should all be combined in a bowl. 2. Cut the dough into scones after kneading it. 3. After that, put them in the air fryer basket with cooking spray on them. 4. Bake the vanilla scones at 185°C for 10 minutes.
**Per Serving:** Calories 24, Fat 1.93g; Sodium 22mg; Carbs 1.23g; Fibre 0.2g; Sugar 0.8g; Protein 0.24g

# Silky Chocolate Pudding with Raspberries

**Prep time: 15 minutes | Cook time: 30 minutes | Serves: 4**

3 tablespoons chia seeds
240 ml unsweetened milk
1 scoop cocoa powder

45 g fresh raspberries
½ teaspoon honey

1. Mix all of the ingredients in a bowl. Let rest for 15 minutes but stir halfway through. 2. Stir again and refrigerate for 30 minutes. Garnish with raspberries. Serve!
**Per Serving:** Calories 254; Fat 7.9g; Sodium 2544mg; Carbs 2g; Fibre 10g; Sugar 6g; Protein 11g

# Raspberry Tart

**Prep time: 5 minutes | Cook time: 20 minutes | Serves: 8**

150g coconut flour
1 teaspoon lime zest, grated
1 teaspoon baking powder
80ml coconut oil, melted

75g raspberries
5 egg whites
65g Erythritol
Cooking spray

1. Combine baking powder, coconut oil, coconut flour, erythritol, and lime zest in an egg mixture. 2. Smooth up the mixture by whisking it. 3. After that, pour the batter into the air fryer basket that has been coated with cooking spray. 4. Place raspberries on top of the batter and bake for 20 minutes at 180°C .
**Per Serving:** Calories 103, Fat 9.18g; Sodium 82mg; Carbs 3.44g; Fibre 1.2g; Sugar 1.8g; Protein 2.7g

# Oatmeal-Carrot Cups

**Prep Time: 10 minutes | Cook Time: 8 to 10 minutes | Serves: 16**

3 tablespoons unsalted butter, at room temperature
55g packed brown sugar
1 tablespoon honey
1 egg white
½ teaspoon vanilla extract

40g finely grated carrot
40g quick-cooking oatmeal
40g whole-wheat pastry flour
½ teaspoon baking soda
30g dried cherries

1. Beat the butter, brown sugar, and honey in a small bowl until well combined, then mix in the egg white, vanilla, and carrot. 2. Stir in the oatmeal, pastry flour, and baking soda. 3. Stir in the dried cherries. 4. Double up 32 mini muffin foil cups to make 16 cups. Fill each with about 4 teaspoons of dough. 5. Working in batches, bake the cookie cups at 175°C for 8 to 10 minutes until light golden brown and just set. 6. Serve warm.
**Per Serving:** Calories 50; Fat 1.73g; Sodium 58mg; Carbs 7.94g; Fibre 0.5g; Sugar 5.22g; Protein 1.08g

# Coconut Pie

**Prep time: 10 minutes | Cook time: 40 minutes | Serves: 8**

120ml coconut cream
3 eggs, beaten
125g coconut flour
1 tablespoon coconut oil, melted

1 tablespoon vanilla extract
1 teaspoon baking powder
3 tablespoons sweetener

1. Combine coconut flour, coconut oil, sweetener, baking powder, and coconut cream with the other ingredients. 2. Next, put the mixture in the air fryer basket and gently press it down. 3. Bake the pie for 40 minutes at 180°C.
**Per Serving:** Calories 124, Fat 10.58g; Sodium 71mg; Carbs 2.99g; Fibre 0.7g; Sugar 1.23g; Protein 4.12g

# Cinnamon Raisin Oatmeal Cookies

**Prep time: 10 minutes | Cook time: 7 minutes | Serves: 18**

55g plus ½ tablespoon vegan margarine
2½ tablespoons nondairy milk, plain and unsweetened
100g organic sugar
½ teaspoon vanilla extract
½ teaspoon plus ⅛ teaspoon ground cinnamon
65g plus 2 tablespoons flour (whole-wheat pastry, gluten-free plain, or plain)

¼ teaspoon sea salt
60g rolled oats
¼ teaspoon baking soda
¼ teaspoon baking powder
2 tablespoons raisins
Cooking oil spray (sunflower, safflower, or refined coconut)

1. Using an electric beater, whip the margarine in a medium bowl until fluffy. 2. Add in the milk, sugar, and vanilla. Stir or whip with beaters until well combined. 3. In a separate bowl, add the cinnamon, flour, salt, oats, baking soda, and baking powder and stir well to combine. Mix the dry mixture to the wet mixture with a wooden spoon until they are well combined. Stir in the raisins. 4. Preheat the air fryer basket (with your 6-inch round, 2-inch deep baking pan inside) to 175°C for 2 minutes. Then, spray the pan lightly with oil. Add the batter onto the pan with a teaspoon, leaving a little room in between each one as they'll probably spread out a bit. Bake at 175°C for about 7 minutes, or until lightly browned. 5. Gently transfer to a cooling rack (or plate), being careful to leave the cookies intact. Repeat as desired, making all of the cookies at once, or keeping the batter on hand in the fridge to be used later (it will keep refrigerated in an airtight container for a week to 10 days).
**Per Serving:** Calories 62; Fat 3g; Sodium 53mg; Carbs 8.7g; Fibre 1g; Sugar 3g; Protein 1g

# Enticing Caramelized Apples

**Prep time: 4 minutes | Cook time: 20 minutes | Serves: 2**

2 apples, any sweet variety
2 tablespoons water
1½ teaspoons coconut sugar
¼ teaspoon cinnamon

Pinch nutmeg
Dash sea salt
Cooking oil spray (sunflower, safflower, or refined coconut)

1. Cut each apple in half (no need to peel) and then remove the core and seeds, doing your best to keep the apple halves intact—because ideally, you want apple halves, not quarters. 2. Place the apples upright in a 15 cm round, 5 cm deep baking pan. Add about 2 tablespoons water to the bottom of the dish to keep the apples from drying out (the apples will sit in the water). 3. Sprinkle evenly the tops of the apples with the sugar, cinnamon, and nutmeg. Give each half a very light sprinkle of sea salt. 4. In short spurts, spray the tops with oil (if you spray too hard, it will make the toppings fly off in a tragic whirlwind). Once moistened, spray the tops again with oil. (This will keep them from drying out.) 5. Bake at 200°C for 20 minutes, or until the apples are very soft and nicely browned on top. Enjoy immediately, plain or topped with granola or ice cream.
**Per Serving:** Calories 112; Fat 1g; Sodium 80mg; Carbs 28g; Fibre 5g; Sugar 21g; Protein 0.6g

# Cinnamon Crisps

### Prep time: 2 minutes | Cook time: 5 to 6 minutes | Serves: 4

1 (20 cm) tortilla, preferably sprouted whole-grain
Cooking oil spray (sunflower, safflower, or refined coconut)

2 teaspoons coconut sugar
½ teaspoon cinnamon

1. Cut the tortilla into 8 triangles (like a pizza). Place on a large plate and spray both sides with oil. 2. Sprinkle the tops evenly with the coconut sugar and cinnamon. In short spurts, spray the tops again with the oil. (If you spray too hard for this step, it will make the powdery toppings fly off!) 3. Place directly in the air fryer basket in a single layer (it's okay if they overlap a little, but do your best to give them space). Fry at 175°C for 5 to 6 minutes, or until the triangles are lightly browned, but not too brown—they're bitter if overcooked. Enjoy warm if possible.
**Per Serving:** Calories 40; Fat 0g; Sodium 83mg; Carbs 7.5g; Fibre 0g; Sugar 1.6g; Protein 1g

# Almonds Doughnuts

### Prep time: 15 minutes | Cook time: 14 minutes | Serves: 6

200g almond flour
2 tablespoons Erythritol
1 egg, beaten

2 tablespoons almond butter, softened
100g heavy cream
1 teaspoon baking powder

1. Combine almond flour, erythritol, egg, almond butter, heavy cream, and baking powder in a mixing dish. Work the dough. 2. Using the cutter, roll up the dough and cut out the donuts. 3. Place the doughnuts in the air fryer basket and fry for 7 minutes on each side at 185°C.
**Per Serving:** Calories 339, Fat 30.44g; Sodium 37mg; Carbs 10.24g; Fibre 5.3g; Sugar 2.61g; Protein 11g

# Apple Cinnamon Puffs

### Prep time: 20 minutes | Cook time: 10 minutes | Serves: 6

**For the Filling**
2 medium apples, cored and finely diced (no need to peel)
2 teaspoons cinnamon
2 tablespoons coconut sugar
⅛ teaspoon sea salt
**For the Vanilla Caramel Sauce**
15 cm segment of a vanilla bean
160g plus 1 tablespoon maple syrup
60ml refined coconut oil (or vegan margarine), plus 2

Cooking oil spray (sunflower, safflower, or refined coconut)
6 large (33 cm x 43 cm) sheets of puff pastry, thawed (see Ingredient Tip)

tablespoons
50g coconut sugar
½ teaspoon sea salt

**To make the filling:** 1. Combine the apples, cinnamon, coconut sugar, and salt in a medium bowl and set aside. 2. Spray an air fryer basket with oil and set aside. Gently unwrap the pastry dough. Remove 6 sheets and carefully set them aside. 3. Wrap the remaining pastry in airtight plastic wrap and place back in the fridge.
**To assemble the puffs:** 1. Remove 1 large sheet of pastry and place on a clean, dry surface. Spray with the oil. Fold it into thirds (the long way, so that you form a long, skinny rectangle). As you go, spray each portion of dry pastry, so the exposed pastry continually gets lightly coated with oil—this will give you a flakier (vs. dry) result. 2. Place ⅓ cup of the apple mixture at the base of the puff pastry rectangle. Fold the bottom of the pastry up and over the mixture. Continue to fold up toward the top, forming it into a triangle as you go. Once you have an apple-filled triangle, place it in the air fryer basket and spray the top with oil. 3. Repeat the steps with the remaining pastry and apple mixture. Note: You'll probably only be able to fit 3 puffs in your air fryer at a time, because you don't want them to overlap. If you don't wish to make a second batch right now, store the pastry wrapped, uncooked puffs in an air-proof container in your fridge and air-fry them within a day or two. 4. Bake at 160°C for 10 minutes, or until very golden-browned.
To make the sauce: 1. Cut lengthwise all the way down the vanilla bean with a sharp knife and pry it open. Scrape out the insides with a table knife and place in a small pot. 2. Add the maple syrup, oil, coconut sugar, and salt to the pot and set to medium-low heat, stirring very well to combine. After bringing the sauce to a boil, reduce the heat to low and simmer gently for 3 to 5 minutes to slightly thickened the sauce.
Transfer the apple puffs to a plate and top with the caramel sauce. Enjoy while warm.
**Per Serving:** Calories 304; Fat 13g; Sodium 344mg; Carbs 46g; Fibre 2g; Sugar 31g; Protein 1.6g

# Crusted Lemon Bars

**Prep time: 15 minutes | Cook time: 25 minutes | Serves: 6**

**For the Crust**
90g whole-wheat pastry flour
2 tablespoons icing sugar

60ml refined coconut oil, melted

**For the Filling**
Cooking oil spray
100g organic sugar
1 packed tablespoon lemon zest
1¾ teaspoons corn flour

⅛ teaspoon sea salt
60ml fresh lemon juice
60g unsweetened, plain applesauce
¾ teaspoon baking powder

**To make the crust:** 1. Stir the icing sugar, flour, and oil together in a small bowl just until well combined. Place the bowl in your fridge.
**To make the filling:** 1. Add the lemon zest and juice, sugar, salt, applesauce, corn flour, and baking powder in a medium bowl. Stir well.
**To assemble the bars:** 1. Lightly spray a 15 cm round, 5 cm-deep baking pan with oil. Then transfer the crust mixture to the bottom of the pan and press gently to form a crust. Place the pan inside your air fryer and bake at 175°C for 5 minutes, or until it becomes slightly firm to the touch. 2. Then spread the lemon filling over the crust. Bake them in your air fryer at 175°C for about 18 to 20 minutes, or until the top is nicely browned. Remove and allow them to cool in the fridge for an hour or more in the fridge. Once firm and cooled, cut them into pieces and serve.
**Per Serving:** Calories 183; Fat 9.5g; Sodium 53mg; Carbs 25g; Fibre 2g; Sugar 12g; Protein 2g

# Strawberry Puffs with Cashew Sauce

**Prep time: 20 minutes | Cook time: 10 minutes | Serves: 8**

**For the Filling**
455g sliced strawberries, fresh or frozen
320g sugar-free strawberry jam (sweetened only with fruit juice)

1 tablespoon corn flour
Cooking oil spray (sunflower, safflower, or refined coconut)
8 large (33 cm x 43 cm) sheets of puff pastry, thawed

**For the Sauce**
130g raw cashew pieces
55g plus 2 tablespoons raw agave nectar
60ml plus 1 tablespoon water
3 tablespoons fresh lemon juice
2 teaspoons (packed) lemon zest

2 tablespoons neutral-flavored oil (sunflower, safflower, or refined coconut)
2 teaspoons vanilla
¼ teaspoon sea salt

**To make the filling:** 1. In a medium bowl, add the strawberries, jam, and corn flour and stir well to combine. Set aside. 2. Prepare the air fryer basket by spraying it with oil and set aside.
**To assemble the puffs:** 1. Gently unwrap the puff pastry. Remove 8 sheets and carefully set them aside. Re-wrap the remaining pastry in airtight plastic wrap and place back in the fridge. 2. Remove 1 large sheet of pastry and place on a clean, dry surface. Spray with the oil. 3. Fold it into thirds so that it forms a long, skinny rectangle. As you go, spray each portion of dry pastry, so the exposed pastry continually gets lightly coated with oil. 4. Place about ⅓ cup of the strawberry mixture at the base of the puff pastry rectangle. Fold the bottom of the pastry up and over the mixture. Continue to fold up toward the top, forming it into a triangle as you go. Once fully wrapped, place it in the air fryer basket and spray the top with oil. 5. Repeat with the remaining pastry and strawberry mixture. Note you'll probably only be able to fit 3 puffs in your air fryer at a time, because you don't want them to overlap. 6. Bake at 160°C for 10 minutes, or until beautifully golden-browned.
**To make the sauce:** 1. Place the cashews, agave, water, lemon juice and zest, oil, vanilla, and salt in a blender. Process until completely smooth and velvety. (Any leftover sauce will keep nicely in the fridge for up to a week.)
Transfer the strawberry puffs to a plate and drizzle with the creamy lemon sauce. If desired, garnish with sliced strawberries. Enjoy while warm.
**Per Serving:** Calories 391; Fat 22g; Sodium 270mg; Carbs 45.6g; Fibre 4g; Sugar 24g; Protein 6g

# Raspberry Streusel Cake

**Prep time: 15 minutes | Cook time: 45 minutes | Serves: 6**

**For the Streusel Topping**
2 tablespoons organic sugar
2 tablespoons neutral-flavored oil (sunflower, safflower, or refined coconut)

**For the Cake**
125g whole-wheat pastry flour
100g organic sugar
1 teaspoon baking powder
1 tablespoon lemon zest
¼ teaspoon sea salt
180ml plus 2 tablespoons unsweetened nondairy milk (plain

**For the Icing**
60g icing sugar
1 tablespoon fresh lemon juice
½ teaspoon lemon zest

30g plus 2 tablespoons whole-wheat pastry flour (or gluten-free plain flour)

or vanilla)
2 tablespoons neutral-flavored oil (sunflower, safflower, or refined coconut)
1 teaspoon vanilla
125g fresh raspberries
Cooking oil spray (sunflower, safflower, or refined coconut)

½ teaspoon vanilla
⅛ teaspoon sea salt

**To make the streusel:** 1. Stir together the sugar, oil, and flour in a small bowl and place in the refrigerator to firm it up and be crumblier later.
**To make the cake:** 1. In a medium bowl, place the flour, sugar, baking powder, zest, and salt. Stir very well, preferably with a wire whisk. Add the milk, oil, and vanilla. Stir them together to combine with a rubber spatula or spoon. Gently stir in the raspberries. 2. Preheat the air fryer for 3 minutes. Spray or coat the insides of a 15 cm round, 5 cm deep baking pan with oil and pour the batter into the pan. 3. Remove the streusel from the fridge and crumble it over the top of the cake batter. Carefully place the cake in the air fryer and bake at 155°C for 45 minutes. A toothpick inserted in the centre shall come out clean (the top should be golden-brown).
**To make the icing:** 1. Stir together the vanilla, icing sugar, lemon juice and zest, and salt in a small bowl. Let the streusel cake cool for about 5 minutes and then slice into 4 pieces and drizzle each with icing. Serve warm if possible. Keep the leftovers in an airtight bowl or resealable bag in your fridge for several days as needed.
**Per Serving:** Calories 311; Fat 10g; Sodium 170mg; Carbs 52g; Fibre 4g; Sugar 29.6g; Protein 5g

# Delightful Apple Crisp

**Prep time: 10 minutes | Cook time: 30 minutes | Serves: 4**

**For the Topping**
2 tablespoons coconut oil
30g plus 2 tablespoons whole-wheat pastry flour (or gluten-free plain flour)

**For the Filling**
220g finely chopped (or thinly sliced) apples (no need to peel)
3 tablespoons water

50g coconut sugar
⅛ teaspoon sea salt

½ tablespoon lemon juice
¾ teaspoon cinnamon

**To make the topping:** 1. In a bowl, combine the oil, flour, sugar, and salt. Mix the ingredients together thoroughly, either with your hands or a spoon. The mixture should be crumbly; if it's not, place it in the fridge until it solidifies a bit.
**To make the filling:** 1. In a 15 cm round, 5 cm-deep baking pan, stir the apples with the water, lemon juice, and cinnamon until well combined. 2. Crumble the chilled topping over the apples. Bake them in your air fryer at 160°C for 30 minutes, or until the chopped apples are tender and the crumbles are crunchy and nicely browned.
Serve immediately on its own or topped with nondairy milk, vegan ice cream, or nondairy whipped cream.
**Per Serving:** Calories 146; Fat 7g; Sodium 79mg; Carbs 21g; Fibre 2g; Sugar 12.7g; Protein 1g

# Simple Vanilla Cheesecake

**Prep Time: 10 minutes | Cook Time: 20 minutes | Serves: 8**

6 full digestive biscuits
2 tablespoons salted butter, melted
300g full-fat cream cheese, softened
100g granulated sugar

2 tablespoons sour cream
1 teaspoon vanilla extract
1 large egg

1. Preheat the air fryer to 150°C. 2. Pulse the biscuits in a food processor fifteen times until finely crushed. Transfer crumbs to a medium bowl. 3. Add butter and mix until the texture is sand-like. Press into a suitable round spring-form pan. 4. Combine cream cheese and sugar, stirring in a large bowl until no lumps remain. Mix in sour cream and vanilla until smooth, then gently mix in egg. 5. Pour batter over crust in pan. Place the pan in the air fryer basket and cook for 20 minutes until top is golden brown. 6. Chill cheesecake in refrigerator at least 4 hours to set before serving.
**Per Serving:** Calories 190; Fat 10.51g; Sodium 231mg; Carbs 18.76g; Fibre 0.4g; Sugar 11.48g; Protein 5g

# Almond-Shortbread Cookies

**Prep Time: 10 minutes | Cook Time: 1 hour 10 minutes | Serves: 8**

115g salted butter, softened
50g granulated sugar
1 teaspoon almond extract

1 teaspoon vanilla extract
250g plain flour

1. Mix cream butter, sugar, and extracts in a large bowl, then gradually add flour, mixing until well combined. 2. Roll dough into a 30 x 5 cm log and wrap in plastic. Chill the dough in refrigerator for at least 1 hour. 3. Preheat the air fryer to 150°C. 4. Slice dough into ½ cm thick cookies. Place in the air fryer basket 5 cm apart, working in batches as needed, and cook for 10 minutes until the edges start to brown. 5. Let cool completely before serving.
**Per Serving:** Calories 196; Fat 8.04g; Sodium 63mg; Carbs 27.07g; Fibre 0.9g; Sugar 3.22g; Protein 3.34g

# Conclusion

The Tower Air Fryer is one of the world's most versatile and advanced cooking appliances, and its large capacity makes it the perfect cooking appliance for the whole family. With its numerous cooking functions, the air fryer allows you to cook virtually anything easily and quickly.

This cookbook contains many simple and delicious Tower Air Fryer recipes and includes easy-to-find ingredients, step-by-step cooking instructions, prep/cook times, and serving suggestions. If you want to make your life easier and more comfortable, then an air fryer is the best appliance for you, saving you time and money. This cookbook lets you select from yummy and easy-to-make breakfast, poultry, lamb, beef, snack, and dessert recipes.

This Tower Air Fryer has user-friendly operating buttons and comes with all the accessories you need to create healthy and delicious meals. This air fryer offers all the helpful cooking functions you need, plus extras such as dehydration, without needing separate appliances.

With its large capacity, you can prepare meals for the whole family or a large group of friends. It's perfect for cooking for special occasions or parties, allowing you to spend quality time with your loved ones rather than toiling away in the kitchen. Need to make nutritious meals, but fast? Then the Tower Air Fryer's got you covered.

Don't worry if you've never used an air fryer before. Simply read through this cookbook alongside the appliance manual, and you'll quickly discover that the Tower Air Fryer is easy to use. You'll be creating delicious, nutritious meals in no time.

Thank you for choosing this cookbook. I hope you enjoy making these recipes as much as we loved creating them. Happy air frying!

# Appendix 1 Measurement Conversion Chart

## VOLUME EQUIVALENTS (LIQUID)

| US STANDARD | US STANDARD (OUNCES) | METRIC (APPROXIMATE) |
|---|---|---|
| 2 tablespoons | 1 fl.oz | 30 mL |
| ¼ cup | 2 fl.oz | 60 mL |
| ½ cup | 4 fl.oz | 120 mL |
| 1 cup | 8 fl.oz | 240 mL |
| 1½ cup | 12 fl.oz | 355 mL |
| 2 cups or 1 pint | 16 fl.oz | 475 mL |
| 4 cups or 1 quart | 32 fl.oz | 1 L |
| 1 gallon | 128 fl.oz | 4 L |

## VOLUME EQUIVALENTS (DRY)

| US STANDARD | METRIC (APPROXIMATE) |
|---|---|
| ⅛ teaspoon | 0.5 mL |
| ¼ teaspoon | 1 mL |
| ½ teaspoon | 2 mL |
| ¾ teaspoon | 4 mL |
| 1 teaspoon | 5 mL |
| 1 tablespoon | 15 mL |
| ¼ cup | 59 mL |
| ½ cup | 118 mL |
| ¾ cup | 177 mL |
| 1 cup | 235 mL |
| 2 cups | 475 mL |
| 3 cups | 700 mL |
| 4 cups | 1 L |

## TEMPERATURES EQUIVALENTS

| FAHRENHEIT(F) | CELSIUS (C) (APPROXIMATE) |
|---|---|
| 225 °F | 107 °C |
| 250 °F | 120 °C |
| 275 °F | 135 °C |
| 300 °F | 150 °C |
| 325 °F | 160 °C |
| 350 °F | 180 °C |
| 375 °F | 190 °C |
| 400 °F | 205 °C |
| 425 °F | 220 °C |
| 450 °F | 235 °C |
| 475 °F | 245 °C |
| 500 °F | 260 °C |

## WEIGHT EQUIVALENTS

| US STANDARD | METRIC (APPROXINATE) |
|---|---|
| 1 ounce | 28 g |
| 2 ounces | 57 g |
| 5 ounces | 142 g |
| 10 ounces | 284 g |
| 15 ounces | 425 g |
| 16 ounces (1 pound) | 455 g |
| 1.5 pounds | 680 g |
| 2 pounds | 907 g |

# Appendix 2 Recipes Index

Printed in Great Britain
by Amazon

39365389R00061